Uniforms and Insignia of the Cossacks

Uniforms and Insignia of the Cossacks in the German Wehrmacht in World War II

Peter Schuster & Harald Tiede

Schiffer Military History
Atglen, PA

I would like to dedicate this book to my friend Nikolai von Lindenau, whose father served in the 1st Cossack Division. Nicolai was murdered on 29 September 1999.
Peter Schuster

Translated from the German by David Johnston
Book Design by Ian Robertson.

Library of Congress Catalog Number: 2003111646

Printed in China.
ISBN: 0-7643-1941-8

This book was originally printed under the title,
Die Uniformen und Abzeichen der Kosaken in der deutschen Wehrmacht
by Klaus D. Patzwall Verlag

Published by Schiffer Publishing Ltd.
4880 Lower Valley Road
Atglen, PA 19310
Phone: (610) 593-1777
FAX: (610) 593-2002
E-mail: info@schifferbooks.com.
Visit our web site at: www.schifferbooks.com
Please write for a free catalog.
This book may be purchased from the publisher.
Please include $3.95 postage.
Try your bookstore first.

In Europe, Schiffer books are distributed by:
Bushwood Books
6 Marksbury Avenue
Kew Gardens
Surrey TW9 4JF
England
Phone: 44 (0) 20 8392-8585
FAX: 44 (0) 20 8392-9876
E-mail: info@bushwoodbooks.co.uk.
Free postage in the UK. Europe: air mail at cost.
Try your bookstore first.

Table of Contents

Introduction

This book differs from those which retell the history of the Cossacks. The fate and sacrifices of the Cossacks have been covered admirably in other works. The purpose of this book is to examine the uniforms and badges of an almost forgotten group of soldiers. When I began my work the task seemed hopeless, because very little material was available. I sought and received help from the veterans group of the XV Cossack Cavalry Corps, specifically Herr E.F. Kamischke and Herr E. Krause.

Herr Harald Tiede, who had been studying this subject for years, joined me as co-author. With the cooperation of former members of many Cossack units and the survivors of deceased members, we collected a great deal of material, which appears in this book. To ensure accuracy, I personally interviewed many former members of the XV Cossack Cavalry Corps. Some questions remain unanswered, perhaps forever. Much has been forgotten in the forty years since the war. What should remain, is the memory of a group of soldiers who bravely carried out the tasks assigned to them: *General* Helmuth von Pannwitz and his Cossacks.

Peter Schuster, Munich 1988

Acknowledgments

I wish to express my gratitude to the following persons and archives, as well as museums, who assisted us in our efforts to assemble an almost complete and accurate description of the uniforms worn by the Cossacks:

Eitel-Friedrich Kamischke (archivist of the XV Cossack Cavalry Corps Veterans Association), Erwin Krause (chairman of the XV Cossack Cavalry Corps Veterans Association, deceased), Otto Münter, Dr. Hermann Blaese, Eva and Klaus Arnheiter, Willi Knocke, Werner Oppermann (deceased), F. Boychevsky, Hartwig Lauts (deceased), Hans Battlehner, Karl-Gottfried Vierkorn, Count Friedrich-Wilhelm von der Schulenburg (deceased), Arthur Künne, Philipp von Schoeller, Stanislav Ausky, Hugo von Senger, Helga Hock, Friedrich Karl Wenzlaff, Dr. Herbert Michner, Nicolai von Lindenau (deceased), Michael Thompson, Anton Budde (deceased) and Brunhilde Kübler.

Thanks to Mr. David Littlejohn, J.R. Angolia and Dr. Klietmann for allowing us to use illustrations from their books.

Archive of the Veterans Association of the Former XV Cossack Cavalry Corps
Bundeaarchiv/Militärarchiv Freiburg
National Archives Washington
Imperial War Museum London
Royal Library Copenhagen
Military History Museum – Rastatt Castle

The majority of the uniforms, headgear, sleeve badges, decorations, documents, pennants, sidearms and photographs are from private collections and were generously made available for this book.

Cossacks in the Imperial Russian Army

This chapter on the uniforms of the Cossacks serving in the Imperial Russian Army is intended to serve as an introduction to the book's main theme. These traditional uniforms influenced the uniforms worn by the Cossacks serving in the *Wehrmacht*. Uniquely Cossack features were incorporated into the design of shoulder straps, cockades, etc. The descriptions of uniforms which follow are from Hans Rottmann's "*Die russische Armee*", and text and photographs from that book are reproduced here.

Uniforms of the Cossacks

Imperial Escort (Konvoy)

The four *sotnia* formed from Kuban and Terek Cossacks wore a uniform derived from the costume of the Caucasian mountain peoples. This consisted of a tall black fur hat with red lining, a short red blouse (*beshmet*) with yellow trim, and over this a long blue caftan (*cherkesska*) with yellow trim and long sleeves, no collar, and a triangular cutout at the neck. Lanyards with the Czar's name on the bottom edge. Caucasian saber on a black strap over the shoulder, Caucasian dagger (*kindshal*) on the belt. Boots with no heels or spurs. The exterior garment was a full-length, sleeveless rider's coat (*burka*) made of black felt without shoulder straps.

Parade Dress: band for decorations on the fur hat. White *beshmet*, red *cherkesska*. A compass on a short braid was worn on the left shoulder. The trumpeters, mounted on white horses, wore thick braids on the breast and sleeves. Officers also wore a red peaked cap with white piping. Silver braid replaced the trim on the hat, *beshmet* and *cherkesska*. The metal cases of the cartridge holders were attached to the *cherkesska* by clips. On horseback the Caucasian saber was buckled on, at all other times it was slung from a gold or silver braid worn over the right shoulder. For parades: silver epaulettes, long revolver cord slung around the neck and right shoulder. The *burka* was only worn by officers in the front, otherwise a coat with red collar patches and shoulder straps with zigzag braid and title.

Bodyguard Cossacks (*Kasaki*)

For parades the regiments wore short blouses of various colors. In combined Cossack regiments the uniforms differed based on the army from which the *sotny* or platoon was recruited. Uniforms were one basic color, with piping on the top of the cap and collar differentiating the units. All of this regiment's units had white piping on the cuffs and shoulder straps. The bodyguard *sotny* of the His Majesty Regiment and the Ural *sotny* bore the name of the Czar. Officers had smooth silver braid and bandoliers of silver braid with piping in the designation color. The bandoliers and belts of the Bodyguard Ataman Cossack Regiment had blue-silver stripes. The bandoliers of the His Majesty and Ataman Cossack Regiments and the Ural *Sotny* were adorned with the name of the Czar. The cartouche had a silver top bearing the Star of St. Andrew.

The dress uniform included long dark blue pants with twin stripes in the designation color. A dark blue blouse with colored piping and shoulder straps was worn as part of the standard uniform. When off duty, officers wore a dark blue outer blouse, which reached to the knees (*chekmen*), with no braid, with tails and colored piping on the collar and cuffs. The Cossack saber was worn suspended from a white leather belt slung over the right shoulder, officers on a braided belt.

The first rank carried lances, but without pennants. The parade saddlecloth was the same color as the blouse with broad white or silver braid on the edge and across the somewhat pointed rear end.

His Majesty's Bodyguard Don Cossack Battery, the Mounted Guard Artillery Brigade

The officers of the brigade had golden aiguillettes and golden stitching similar to that of the rest of the guards artillery. Gold bandolier with monogram. Cartridge box with silver cover, on it the Star of St. Andrew and crossed cannon. Dress uniform included long dark blue pants with red stripes. Parade saddlecloth dark green with yellow (gold) trim.

Army Cossacks

On parade the Cossack armies wore black fur caps (*papachka*) of various styles. Even within units there were variations in shape and size. The cap body was sewn across and at the bottom with silver braid or white galloon. The short blouse was closed at the front with hooks. Enlisted men wore braiding of white galloon with colored inner stripes. The officers wore simple silver braiding on the collars and cuffs of their blouses. The silver bandolier was worn with the buckle and slide facing the chest. The cartouche had a black leather cover trimmed with silver braid and adorned with the double eagle. Officers wore spurs, while the enlisted men did not. The enlisted man's leathers were white. The service uniform worn by officers and enlisted men included a gray-green smock with a row of white metal buttons.

As an identifying feature, every Cossack was permitted to carry a Cossack saber (*shashka*) of any style decorated as he wished. Consequently it was not uncommon to see old pieces, either inherited or captured, in use, sometimes with expensive silver fittings.

When off duty or in the field, personnel were allowed to wear fur caps in the style of their choice in any natural color (except for white, and in the field except for black) with cloth lining. Black fur caps with red or pale blue lining were always worn only on parade and with the standard uniform. The long caftan (*cherkesska*), with long white sleeves and no collar, could be worn in any shade of brown, gray or black and *cherkesskas* of the same color were only worn on parade or with the standard uniform. On the shoulder straps of the cavalry regiments was the first letter of the regiment's name, on those of the Plastun battalions, whose caftans were shorter, the battalion number. On parade, shirts with standing collars (*beshmet* or *archalup*) in the designation color were worn beneath the caftan. While on duty and everyday, the shirt could be of various colors, with white and black predominating. Bright colors were avoided in the field. In winter, hoods (*bashlyk*) were attached to the back for parades.

The officer's parade uniform included braid trimming on the cap and caftan, the cartridge holders on the breast, the shirt and the hood. In winter the collar cutout of the *cherkesska* could be lined with fur. Furthermore, as everyday wear officers wore a gray-green smock similar to those worn by the officers of other units, with a peaked cap in the color of the parade caftan with trim stripes and piping in the designation color. The Caucasian saber was buckled on when on horseback and worn over the right shoulder when on foot. On parade the belts worn by officers, like the compass cord worn over the left shoulder, was made of braid, at all other times of leather with metal fittings. The long Caucasian dagger was suspended from a narrow belt. Spurs were not worn. The enlisted men always wore the *burka* in place of a coat.

Two Czarist officers and a volunteer (right). The Cossack officer in the center is wearing the shoulder straps of a Harungee (lowest grade of the Lieutenant rank in the Czarist army) on his cherkesska.

Parade uniform of a Cossack of the Imperial Escort.

Cossack circa 1900.

Kasaken
Leib-Garde-Ural-Kasak. Paradeunif.
Orenburg-Kasak.
Unteroffizier der L.-G.-Ataman-Kasaken. Paradeunif.
Offizier der Kuban-Kasaken. Parade.
Offizier der Astrachan-Kasaken. Paradeunif.
Ural-Kasak. Dienstunif.
Don-Kasak mit Reg.-Zeichen d. 17. Regts. Paradeunif.
Transbaikal-Kasak.
Offizier der Amur-Kasaken. Gewöhnl. Uniform.

Kasaken.
Don-Kasaken-Offizier.
Don-Kasak.
Don-Kasak.
Dienstuniform.
Orenburg-Kasak.
Ural-Kasak.
Astrachan-Kasak.
(nur Offiziere)
Kuban-Fuß-Kasak.
(nur Offiziere)
Kuban-Kasak zu Pferde.
(nur Offiziere)
Terek-Kasak.
Sibir. Kasak.
Semiretschensk-Kasak.
Transbaikal-Kasak.
Amur-Kasak.
Ussuri-Kasak.
Dagestan-Reiter-Regt.
Ossetiner Reiter-Regt.
Kasaken-Sommeruniform.
Garde-Don-Kasaken-Battr.
Don-Kasaken-Battr.
Orenburg-Kasaken-Battr.
(nur Offiziere)
Kuban-Kasaken-Battr.

Dagestani Cavalry Regiment (Temir-Chan-Shura)

The uniform was similar to that of the Caucasian Cossacks, however the parade cap top and *beshmet* were white. The trim stripes and piping on the officer's peaked caps were also white, the facing on the coat collars of the officers were white with red trim, however the shoulder straps and the parade *bashlyk* were red. The silver officers braid had a red central stripe.

Ossetian Cavalry Half-Regiment (*Stavropoli*)

Similar to the Caucasian Cossacks, but the parade caftan was black-gray, badges pale blue, *bashlyk* white.

Turkmenian Irregular Cavalry Half-Regiment (*Kaschi bei As-chabad*)

Whereas the cut of the officer's uniform was similar to that of the Caucasian Cossacks, consisting of a black *cherkesska*, yellow *beshmet* and white *bashlyk*, enlisted men wore a white-, dark red-, black- and yellow-striped caftan with yellow shoulder straps, collarless yellow shirt with red galloon, broad black belt and a large black cone-shaped fur cap.

Officers of the Kuban Cossacks in their cherkesskas.

A Cossack officer in a light cherkesska, circa 1910.

Flags and Standards

Each Cossack regiment or battalion had a flag or standard bearing all the decorations, such as flag stripes, George Cross, inscriptions, etc, which had been won by the unit. As well, the Cossack armies had so-called "Army Flags". The upper part of pennants of the Cossack *sotnia* were the color of the shoulder straps of the army of which they were part, the lower part the color of the Sotny (1st *Sotny* red, 2nd blue, 3rd white, 4th green, 5th yellow and 6th brown). Furthermore, the Cossacks used large rectangular flags in the army color with white numbers or letters as regimental emblems. An exception was the 17th Don Cossack Regiment, which had a black flag with a white death's head and the legend, "I believe in the resurrection of the dead and eternal life in the future", on one side and a number on the other. This was done in memory of General Baklanov, whose name the regiment bore, who was always accompanied by this symbol during his campaigns of conquest in the Caucasus.

Cossack Units in the Second World War

Cossack Units on the Eastern Front on 25 March 1943:

Army Group A:

- Cossack Regiment Platov
- Cossack Regiment Kuban
- 1st and 2nd Cossack Companies with the 97th Light Infantry Division

Army Group South:

- Cossack Regiment Jungschultz
- III (Cossack) Battalion/57th Security Regiment
- Cossack Battalion 213
- Cossack Battalion 403
- Cossack Battalion I/444
- Cossack Battalion II/444
- Cossack Battalion I/454
- Cossack Battalion II/454
- Cossack Battalion 557 (Don)
- Cossack Battalion 558 (Kuban)
- Cossack Training Battalion
- Cossack Company (Motorized) with the 3rd Panzer Corps
- Cossack Company 404
- Cossack Battery 553

Army Group North:

- Cossack Troop 655

Army Group Center:

- Cossack Battalion 433
- Cossack Battalion 600
- Cossack Battalion 622
- Cossack Battalion 623
- Cossack Battalion 624
- Cossack Battalion 625
- Cossack Battalion 631
- 1st and 2nd Cossack Companies 137
- Cossack Company 638

Other Cossack Units

This list of Cossack units makes no claims to completeness. There were many small Cossack units which, though not part of the 1st Cossack Division, were employed within the division as security or combat units.

1.) Cossack Training and Replacement Regiment (later Volunteer Cossack Cadre Regiment 5), which also included the Young Cossack School. The training and replacement regiment had a strength of 10,000 to 15,000 men. In the autumn of 1943 it was transferred to various training camps in Germany and France. In 1944 it was employed in strengthening the *Westwall* (Siegfried Line) fortifications and toward the end of the year was employed against French *Maquisards* on the Plateau de Langres.

2.) Cavalry Unit Trubchevsky. At the beginning of 1943 it formed the 5th (Heavy) Troop of the Boeselanger Cavalry Unit.

3.) 7th Cavalry Regiment

4.) Cossack Battalion 69 (joined the 1st Cossack Division in November 1944)

5.) 1st and 2nd Cossack Troop 82 with the XXX Panzer Corps

6.) 1st Ost/131 and 2nd Ost/131. Both units belonged to the 131st Infantry Division and were called Eastern Cavalry. The members of this unit liked to call themselves Cossacks, although most of them were Ukrainians.

7.) East Cavalry Battalion 285 (Security Division 285)

8.) Cavalry Regiment 360 (ultimately Grenadier Regiment 360)

9.) Cossack Battalion 428 (joined the 1st Cossack Division in January 1945)

10.) Battalion 570

11.) Don Cossack Troop 583 (joined the 1st Cossack Division shortly before the end of the war).
12.) Cossack Battalion 669
13.) Cossack Battalion 126
14.) Cossack Battalion 161
15.) 9th Cossack Troop of Bicycle Regiment 4
16.) 1st and 2nd Cossack Troops 82 of the 3rd Panzer Division
17.) 1st Sinegorski Ataman RRT
18.) A motorized Cossack company of the III Panzer Corps
19.) A Cossack reconnaissance battalion (part of the 97th Light Infantry Division)
20.) Cossack Troop 287 of the Special Purpose Corps Headquarters (Special Unit 287)

Command List of the 1st Cossack Division
(as of Sept.-Oct. 1943)

Division commander:	*Generalmajor* Helmuth von Pannwitz
IA (Operations Officer):	*Oberstleutnant* von Schultz
IB (Logistics Officer):	*Major* Rohahn
IC (Intelligence Officer):	*Major* Count zu Eltz
IIA:	*Rittmeister* Himighoffen
III:	*Kriegsgericht* Dr. Müller
IVA:	*Intendanturrat* Hecht
IVB:	*Oberstabsarzt* d.R. Dr. Grass
IVC:	*Stabsveterinär* Dr. Schwerdtfeger
1st Cossack Cavalry Brigade (Don)	
Commander:	*Oberst* Baron Hans von Wolff
IA:	*Rittmeister* von Abel
IIA:	*Oberleutnant* von Schoeller
Don Cossack Cavalry Regiment 1	
Commander:	*Oberstleutnant* d.R. Burggraf von Dohna, *Oberst* Wagner (until February 1945)
Commander 1st Battalion:	*Rittmeister* Dienenthal
Commander 2nd Battalion:	*Rittmeister* d.R. Mattern
Siberian Cossack Cavalry Regiment 2	
Commander:	*Oberstleutnant* Baron von Nolcken
Commander 1st Battalion:	*Rittmeister* Schreiber
Commander 2nd Battalion:	*Rittmeister* Behm
Kuban Cossack Cavalry Regiment 4	
Commander:	*Oberstleutnant* Baron Paul von Wolff
Commander 1st Battalion:	*Rittmeister* Mach
Commander 2nd Battalion:	*Rittmeister* d.R. von Laer
1st Mounted Cossack Artillery Battalion 55	
Commander:	*Hauptmann* von Eisenhart-Rothe
2nd Cossack Cavalry Brigade (Caucasus)	
Commander:	*Oberst* von Bosse
IA:	*Rittmeister* Freise
IIA:	*Oberleutnant* Count von Bismarck-Bohlen

Kuban Cossack Cavalry Regiment 3

Commander:	*Oberstleutnant d.R.* Jungschulz von Roebern
Commander 1st Battalion:	*Rittmeister* Count von der Schulenburg
Commander 2nd Battalion:	*Rittmeister* Langfeldt

Don Cossack Cavalry Regiment 5

Commander:	*Oberstleutnant* Kononov
Liaison Officer:	*Rittmeister d.R.* Count von Rittberg
Commander 1st Battalion:	*Rittmeister* Cherbakov
Commander 2nd Battalion:	*Rittmeister* Borisov

Terek Cossack Cavalry Regiment 6

Commander:	*Major d.R.* von Kalben
Commander 1st Battalion:	*Rittmeister* Gunst
Commander 2nd Battalion:	*Rittmeister* Friedrich

2nd Mounted Cossack Artillery Battalion 55

Commander:	*Hauptmann* Count von Kottulinsky

Division Units

Division Reconnaissance Battalion 55

Commander:	*Rittmeister* Weil

Cossack Combat Engineer Battalion 55

Commander:	*Hauptmann* Jans

Cossack Signals Battalion 55

Cossack Medical Battalion 55

Commander:	*Oberstabsarzt d.R.* Dr. Grass
1st Medical Company:	*Stabsarzt* Dr. von der Heide
2nd Medical Company:	*Stabsarzt d.R.* Dr. Maaßen
Field Hospital:	*Stabsarzt* Dr. Bogdanoff
Division Supply Chief:	*Rittmeister d.R.* Bröcker
Veterinary Company:	Stabsveterinär Dr. Gans

Cossack Replacement Regiment:

Commander:	*Oberstleutnant* Stabenow
Adjutant:	*Oberleutnant d.R.* von Scharfenberg

Command List of the XV Cossack Cavalry Corps
(as of 25 Feb. 1945)

Commanding General:	*Generalleutnant* Helmuth von Pannwitz
Commander:	*Oberst* Wagner
Chief of Staff:	*Oberstleutnant d.R.* von Steinsdorff
IA:	*Rittmeister d.R.* Count von Schweidnitz
IB:	*Major i.G.* Schneider (Quartermaster)
IC:	*Major* Count zu Eltz
IIA:	*Major* Himmighofen
III:	Kriegsgericht Dr. Müller
IVA:	*Intendanturrat* Hecht
IVB:	*Oberfeldsarzt* d.R. Dr. Grass
IVC:	*Oberstabsveterinär* Dr. Schwerdtfeger
Liaison Officer to the Ataman Headquarters:	*Oberst* d.R. von Renteln
Corps Reconnaissance Battalion:	*Major* Weil
Corps Pioneer Officer:	*Major* Jans
Corps Signals Officer:	*Major* Schmidt

1st Cossack Cavalry Division	
Commander:	*Oberst* von Bath (Deputy: *Oberst* Wagner, then *Oberst* Körner)
IA:	*Major i.G* Schlie
IIA:	*Major* Gündel
Don Cossack Cavalry Regiment 1	
Commander:	*Major* Dienenthal
Siberian Cossack Cavalry Regiment 2	
Commander:	*Oberst* Baron von Nolcken
Kuban Cossack Cavalry Regiment 4	
Commander:	*Oberstleutnant* von Klein
Cossack Artillery Regiment 1 (in formation)	
Designated commander:	*Major* von Eisenhart-Rothe
2nd Cossack Cavalry Division	
Commander:	*Oberst* von Schultz
IA:	*Major* i.G. Rojahn
IIA:	*Rittmeister* Count von Schmettow
Kuban Cossack Cavalry Regiment 3	
Commander:	*Oberstleutnant* d.R. Lehmann
Don Cossack Cavalry Regiment 5	
Commander:	*Oberstleutnant* Borisov
IC:	*Major* Count zu Eltz
Terek Cossack Cavalry Regiment 6	
Commander:	*Oberstleutnant* Prince zu Salm-Horstmar
Cossack Artillery Regiment 2 (in formation)	

Plastun Brigade in the XV Cossack Cavalry Corps
(3rd Cossack Division in formation, state as of 25 Feb. 1945)

Commander:	*Oberst* Kononov until March 1945, then *Oberst* von Renteln
Liaison Officer:	*Major* d.R. Count von Rittberg
Plastun Regiment 7, Commander:	*Oberstleutnant* Borisov
Plastun Regiment 8, Commander:	*Major* Sakharov
Reconnaissance Battalion, Commander:	*Rittmeister* Bondarenko

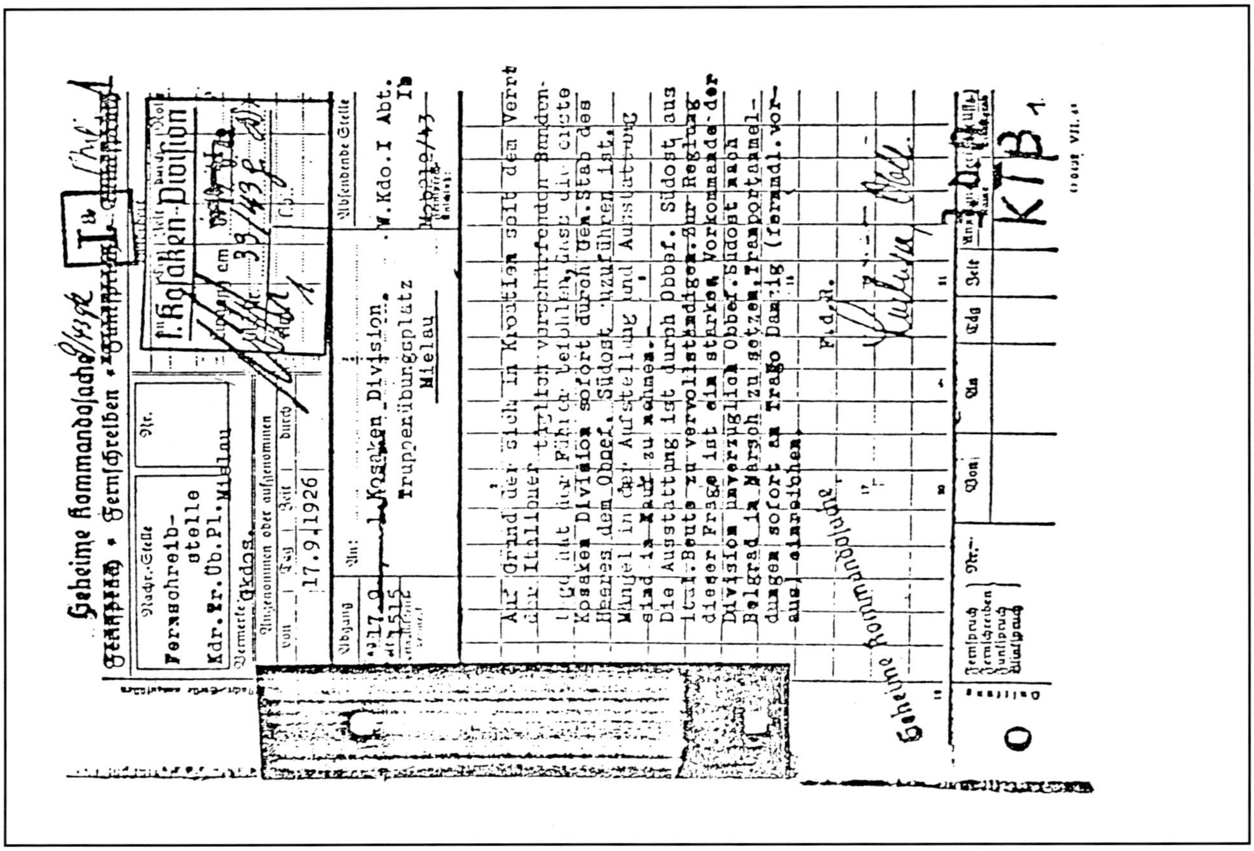

Geheime Kommandosache

Fernspruch • Fernschreiben

Nachr.-Stelle: Fernschreibstelle Kdr. Tr. Üb. Pl. Mielau

Vermerke: Gkdos.

Angenommen oder aufgenommen: 17.9. 1926

I. Kosaken-Division

Abgang: 17.9. 1515

An: 1. Kosaken Division Truppenübungsplatz Mielau

Absendende Stelle: W.Kdo.I Abt. Ib

Auf Grund der sich in Kroatien seit dem Verrat der Italiener täglich verschärfenden Bandenlage hat der Führer befohlen, dass die erste Kosaken Division sofort durch Gen.Stab des Heeres dem Obbef. Südost zuzuführen ist. Mängel in der Aufstellung und Ausstattung sind in Kauf zu nehmen.

Die Ausstattung ist durch Obbef. Südost aus ital. Beute zu vervollständigen. Zur Reglung dieser Frage ist ein starkes Vorkommando der Division unverzüglich Obbef. Südost nach Belgrad in Marsch zu setzen. Transportanmeldungen sofort an Trago Danzig (fernmdl. voraus) einreichen.

F.d.R.

Geheime Kommandosache

KTB 1

Marching order of the 1st Cossack Division dated 17 September 1943.

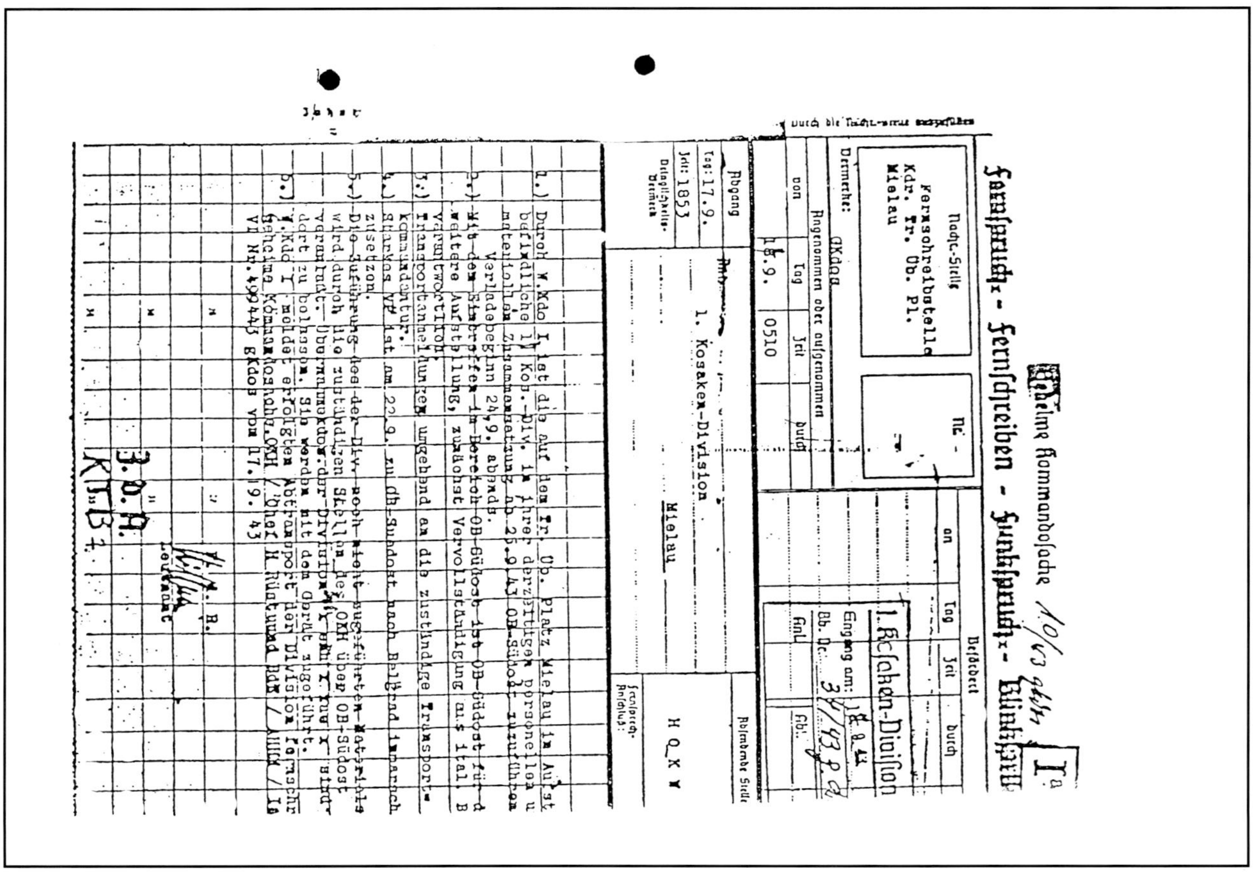

Geheime Kommandosache

Fernspruch – Fernschreiben – Funkspruch – Blinkspruch

Nachr.-Stelle: Fernschreibstelle Kdr. Tr. Üb. Pl. Mielau

Vermerke: GKdos

Angenommen oder aufgenommen: 18.9. 0510

1. Kosaken-Division Eingang am: 18.9.43 Bb. Nr. 34/43 g.K.

Abgang: Tag: 17.9. Zeit: 1853

An: 1. Kosaken-Division Mielau

Absendende Stelle: H Q K W

1.) Durch W.Kdo I. ist die auf dem Tr. Üb. Platz Mielau im Aufstellung befindliche 1. Kos.-Div. in ihrer derzeitigen personellen und materiellen Zusammensetzung ab 25.9.43 OB-Südost zuzuführen. Verladebeginn 24.9. abends.

2.) Mit dem Eintreffen im Bereich OB-Südost ist OB-Südost für die weitere Aufstellung, zunächst Vervollständigung aus ital. Beute verantwortlich.

3.) Transportanmeldungen umgehend an die zuständige Transportkommandantur.

4.) Starkes VK ist am 22.9. zu OB-Südost nach Belgrad in Marsch zu setzen.

5.) Die Zuführung des der Div. noch nicht zugeführten Materials wird durch die zuständigen Stellen des OKH über OB-Südost veranlasst. Übernahmekdos. der Division sind dort zu belassen. Sie werden mit dem Gerät zugeführt.

6.) W.Kdo I meldet erfolgten Abtransport der Division fernschriftlich Geheime Kommandosache. OKH / Chef H Rüst und BdE / AHA / Ia VI Nr. 499443 gKdos vom 17.9.43

I.A.

Leutnant

3.D.A.

KTB 1

1. Kosaken-Division ... Kommandosache 13/43 gK **Ia** 8

G l i e d e r u n g d e r 1. K o s a k e n - D i v.

DIVISIONS-STAB (mot)

Propagandazug
Feldgend.Trupp a mot
Gendarmerie-Wachzug
Trompeterkorps (ber.)

I. KOSAKEN-REITER-BRIGADE

Stab (mot)

DONKOSAKEN-REITER-RGT. 1

Stab
Nachr.Zug
9.(schw.) Schwadron { 2 Züge mit je 3 m.Pak)
2 " " je 4 m.Werfer)

I.Abteilung
Stab
Nachr.Staffel
4 Schwadronen

II.Abteilung
Stab
Nachr.Staffel
4 Schwadronen

1.-3. u. 5.-7. Schwd.
(3 Züge zu je 3 l.M.G./1 Trupp mit 2 l.W.)
4. u. 8. Schwd.
(2 Züge zu je 4 s.M.G./1 Zug mit 4 m.W.)

SIBIRKOSAKEN-REITER-RGT. 2

Stab
Nachr.Zug
9.(schw.) Schwadron { 2 Züge mit je 3 m.Pak)
2 " " je 4 m.Werfer)

I.Abteilung
Stab
Nachr.Staffel
4 Schwadronen

II.Abteilung
Stab
Nachr.Staffel } mot
4 Schwadronen (Radf.)

1.-3. Schwd.
(3 Züge zu je 3 l.M.G./1 Trupp mit 2 l.W.)
4. Schwd.
(2 Züge zu je 4 s.M.G./1 Zug mit 4 m.W.)

5.-7. Schwd.
(3 Radf.Schwd. zu 3 Zügen mit je 3 l.M.G. u. 1 l.W.)
8. Schwd.
(2 Züge zu je 4 s.M.G./1 Zug mit 4 m.W.)

KUBANKOSAKEN-REITER-RGT. 4

Stab
Nachr.Zug

KUBANKOSAKEN-REITER-RGT. 4

Stab
Nachr.Zug
9.(schw.) Schwadron (2 Züge mit je 3 m.Pak)
(2 Züge mit je 4 m.Werfer)

I.Abteilung
Stab
Nachr.Staffel
4 Schwadronen

II.Abteilung
Stab
Nachr.Staffel
4 Schwadronen

1.-3. u. 5.-7. Schwd.
(3 Züge zu je 3 l.M.G./1 Trupp mit 2 l.W.)

4. u. 8. Schwd.
(2 Züge zu je 4 s.M.G./1 Zug mit 4 m.W.)

I. reit.KOSAKEN-ARTILLERIE-ABT.

Stab
Stabs-Batterie
3 Battr. mit je 4 l.F.K.18

II. KOSAKEN-REITER-BRIGADE

Stab (mot)

KUBANKOSAKEN-REITER-RGT. 3

Stab
Nachr.Zug
9.(schw.) Schwadron (2 Züge mit je 3 m.Pak)
(2 " " je 4 m.Werfer)

I.Abteilung
Stab
Nachr.Staffel
4 Schwadronen

II.Abteilung
Stab
Nachr.Staffel
4 Schwadronen

1.-3. u. 5.-7. Schwd.
(3 Züge zu je 3 l.M.G./1 Trupp mit 2 l.W.)

4. u. 8. Schwd.
(2 Züge zu je 4 s.M.G./1 Zug mit 4 m.W.)

DONKOSAKEN-REITER-RGT. 5

Stab
Nachr.Zug
9.(schw.) Schwadron (2 Züge mit je 3 m.Pak)
(2 Züge mit je 4 m.Werfer)

I.Abteilung
Stab
Nachr.Staffel
4 Schwadronen

II.Abteilung
Stab
Nachr.Staffel
4 Schwadronen
} mot (Radf.)

1.-3. Schwd.
(3 Züge zu je 3 l.M.G./1 Trupp mit 2 l.W.)

4. Schwd.
(2 Züge zu je 4 s.M.G./1 Zug mit 4 m.W.,

5.-7. Schwd.
(3 Radf.Schwd. zu 3 Zügen mit je 3 l.M.G. u. 1 l.W.)

8. Schwd.
(2 Züge zu je 4 s.M.G./1 Zug mit 4 m.W.)

TEREKKOSAKEN-REITER-RGT. 6

Stab
Nachr.Zug
9.(schw.) Schwadron (2 Züge mit je 3 m.Pak) (2 Züge mit je 4 m.Werfer)

I.Abteilung

Stab
Nachr.Staffel
4 Schwadronen

II.Abteilung

Stab
Nachr.Staffel
4 Schwadronen

1.-3. u. 5.-7. Schwd.
(3 Züge zu je 3 l.M.G./1 Trupp mit 2 l.W.)

4. u. 8. Schwd.
(2 Züge zu je 4 s.M.G./1 Zug mit 4 m.W.)

II. reit.KOSAKEN-ARTILLERIE-ABT.

Stab
Stabs-Batterie
3 Battr. mit je 4 l.F.K.18

KOS.NACHRICHTEN-ABT.

Stab
1.Fernsprechkomp.
2.Fernsprechkomp.
3.Funk-Komp. (t mot)
le.Nachr.Kolonne

KOS.PIONIER-BTL.

Stab
mit le.Kol.
Brückenkolonne C
1.Kos.Pi.Komp.
2. " " " (mot)
3.Kos.Pi.Komp.
4.Kos.Bau-Komp. } bereits aufgestellt. Etatisierungsantrag gestellt

---

VERSORGUNGS - TRUPPEN

Nachschubtruppen

Stab
1 Kraftfahrkompanie (90 to)
3 Fahrschwadronen (zu je 60 to)
1 Nachschubkompanie

Verwaltungstruppen

Verpflegungsamt
Bäckerei-Komp.
Schlächterei-Komp.

Sanitätstruppen

2 Sanitäts-Komp. b
2 Krankenkraftwagenzüge

Veterinärtruppen

1 Veterinär-Komp.
1 Pfd.Trsp.Kol. (mot)

Ordnungstruppen

1 Feldgendarmerietrupp a (mot)
- zum Div.Stab -

Kraftfahrparktruppen

1 [illegible]
1 [illegible] } [illegible]

Feldpostamt (beantragt)

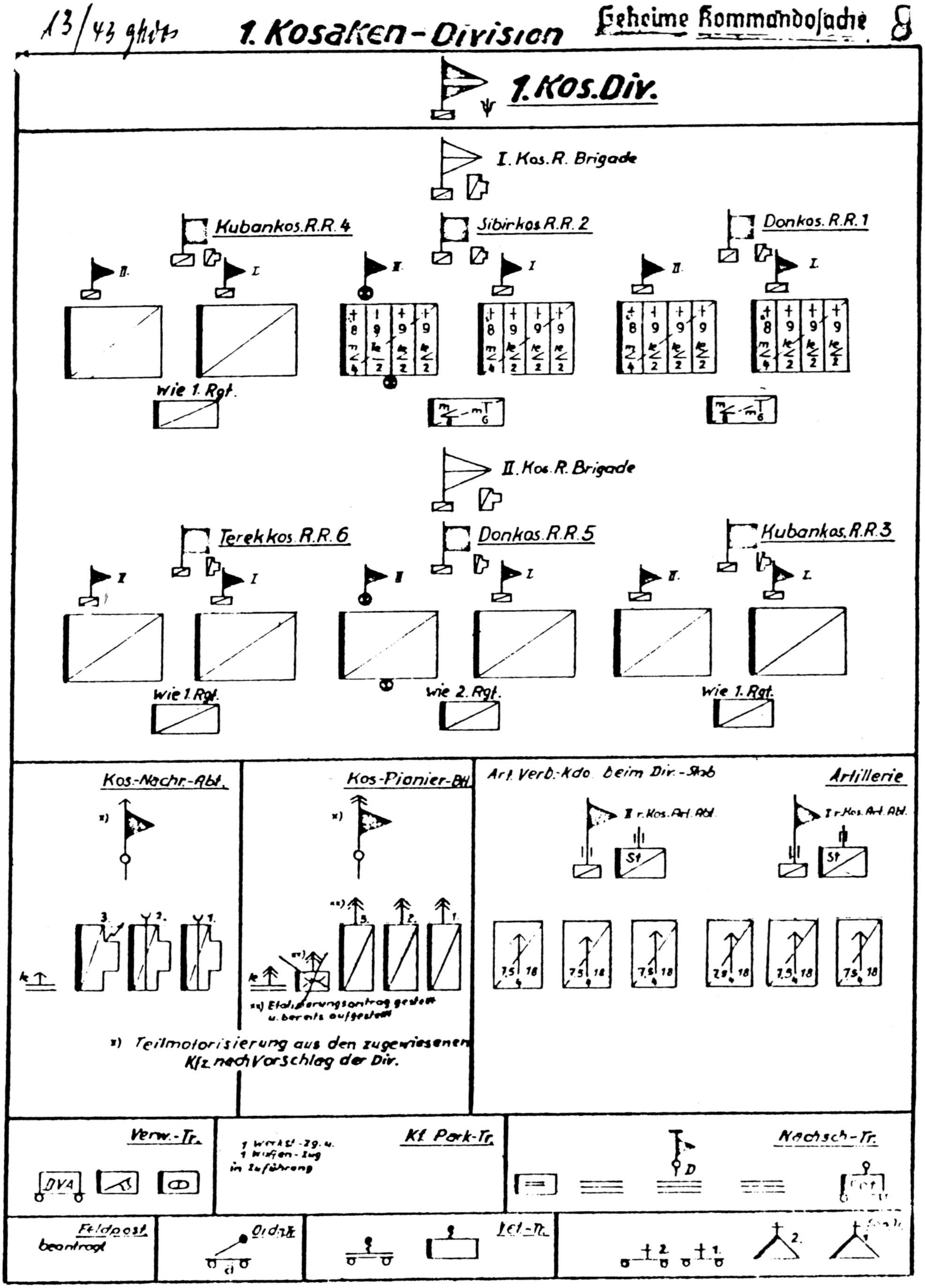
13/43 g.Kdos
1. Kosaken-Division
Geheime Kommandosache
1. Kos.Div.
I. Kos.R. Brigade
Kubankos.R.R.4
Sibirkos.R.R.2
Donkos.R.R.1
wie 1. Rgt.
II. Kos.R. Brigade
Terekkos.R.R.6
Donkos.R.R.5
Kubankos.R.R.3
wie 1. Rgt.
wie 2. Rgt.
wie 1. Rgt.
Kos-Nachr.-Abt.
Kos-Pionier-Btl.
Art. Verb.-Kdo. beim Div.-Stab
Artillerie
I r. Kos. Art. Abt.
I r. Kos. Art. Abt.
St
St
x) Teilmotorisierung aus den zugewiesenen Kfz. nach Vorschlag der Div.
Verw.-Tr.
DVA
Kl. Park-Tr.
in Zuführung
Nachsch.-Tr.
Feldpost
beantragt
Tel.-Tr.

1. KOSAKEN-DIVISION
IIa

O.U., den 17. Oktober 1943 — Ia

Eingang am: 17.10.43
Bearb. Abt.: [illegible]

Stärkemeldung

Stichtag: 15. 1o. 1943

Div. Truppenteil:	Dtsch. Rahmenpersonal				Kosaken			Sdf.		Pferde	Fahrzeuge	Kfz.					
	Offz.	Beamt.	Uffz.	Mannsch.	Offz.	Uffz.	Mannsch.	R/Z	G			Kr.Rad	Pkw.	Lkw.	Om.	Anh.	[illegible]
						7	8					13	14	15	16	17	18
Stab 1. Kos.-Div.	25	1o	66	138	6	1	59	4	1	76	–	13	14	9	–	–	–
Div.Kw.Werkst.Zug	–	1	3	16	–	–	6	–	–	–	–	–	1	4	–	–	–
Betreuungszug	1	–	4	6	5	1	1o	2	–	–	–	–	3	4	–	1	–
Stab 1.Kos.Rtr.Brig.	5	–	8	22	2	–	23	1	–	4	–	5	3	1	–	–	–
Stab 2.Kos.Rtr.Brig.	5	–	7	23	–	–	3	1	–	4	–	5	3	1	–	–	–
Donkos. Reiter Rgt. 1	17	2	1oo	166	2•	163	1524	2	5	1269	282	2	2	3	–	–	2
Sib.Kos.Rtr.Rgt. 2	21	2	125	14o	25	146	1588	2	1	824	143	5	6	3	–	–	2
Kubankos.Rtr.Rgt. 3	16	2	119	126	24	141	1623	–	5	1243	272	2	2	3	–	–	2
Kubankos.Rtr.Rgt. 4	15	4	111	162	27	134	1588	2	7	1292	315	2	2	3	–	–	3
Donkos. Rtr.Rgt. 5	16	3	14o	155	19	135	1553	3	4	812	225	7	6	16	–	–	2
Terekkos. Rtr. Rgt. 6	15	3	113	148	22	142	1599	3	8	1294	257	2	2	3	–	–	2
I.reit.Kos.Art.Abt.	15	1	76	158	3	22	496	–	4	688	142	1	1	1	–	–	–
II.r. Kos.Art.Abt.	14	1	81	164	6	22	5•7	–	6	7o9	141	–	1	1	–	–	–
Kos. Nachr. Abt.	14	1	184	629	4	22	3•5	1	1	453	145	4	1o	13	1	–	–
Kos. Pi.-Btl.	5	1	75	65	3	47	836	–	3	446	15o	6	4	6	–	1	–
Div.-Nachsch.Truppe	12	1	46	65	2o	72	924	–	3	718	372	4	2	29	–	–	–
Vetr.-Komp.	3	1	22	128	–	1	86	–	–	58	21	2	2	1o	–	2	–
Pferde Transp. Kol.	1	–	7	24	–	–	21	–	–	–	–	4	1	11	–	–	–
Bäckerei-Kompanie	1	1	15	15	1	1	144	–	1	67	29	–	–	–	–	–	–
Schlächterei-Komp.	1	1	6	13	1	2	47	–	1	22	1o	–	–	–	–	–	–
1. San.-Komp.	3	1	1o	15	1	7	145	–	1	53	24	–	1	–	–	–	–
2. San.-Komp.	4	1	9	12	3	7	142	–	2	42	18	–	1	–	–	–	–
Div.-Verpfl.-Amt	–	4	8	12	–	–	12	–	–	–	–	–	1	7	–	–	–
Feld.-Wachzug	1	–	29	2	1	12	69	–	2	17	–	2	2	–	–	–	–
1. Kr.Kr.-Zug	1	–	5	21	–	–	16	–	1	–	–	–	–	15	–	–	–
2. Kr.Kr.-Zug	1	–	5	2o	–	–	17	–	1	–	–	–	–	–	–	–	–
												–	1	15	San.-Kraftw.		
	213	41	1374	246o	193	1o78	13343	21	57	1oo91	2546	66	71	158	1	4	13

KTB

Knight's Cross Wearers of the 1st Cossack Division and XV Cossack Cavalry Corps

Generalleutnant Helmuth von Pannwitz, Knight's Cross on 4 September 1941 while serving as commander of Reconnaissance Battalion 45 with the rank of *Oberstleutnant*.
Oak Leaves on 23 December 1942 (167th) while commander of Battle Group von Pannwitz with the rank of *Oberst*. Von Pannwitz commanded the 1st Cossack Division and later the XV Cossack Cavalry Corps. The photo was taken when he was an *Oberst*.

Oberst Count von Wolff, Knight's Cross on 13 July 1940 while serving as commander of I Battalion, 8th Rifle Regiment with the rank of *Hauptmann*.
Oak Leaves on 16 January 1942 (61st) while commander of I Battalion, 28th Rifle Regiment in the 8th Panzer Division with the rank of *Hauptmann*.
Oberst von Wolff was the commander of the 1st Cossack Cavalry Brigade Don from 1943 to January 1944.

Oberst Karl-Walrad Prince zu Salm-Horstmar. Knight's Cross on 19 February 1942 while serving as commander of Reconnaissance Battalion 123 with the rank of *Rittmeister*. Oberst Prince zu Salm was commander of the Terek Cossack Cavalry Regiment 6 from October 1944 to May 1945.

Oberst d.R. Ewert von Renteln. Knight's Cross on 13 January 1945 while serving as commander of Cossack Grenadier Regiment 360 with the rank of *Oberstleutnant*.
Oberst von Renteln was the liaison officer to the Ataman headquarters from the beginning of 1945 until May 1945.

Major Erich Dienenthal. Knight's Cross on 14 January 1941 as acting commander of the 2nd (Bicycle) Company of the Div. Reconnaissance Battalion 45 with the rank of *Oberleutnant*.
Major Dienenthal was the commander of the 1st Battalion of the Don Cossack Cavalry Regiment 1 from May 1943 to February 1945. He commanded the Don Cossack Cavalry Regiment 1 from February to May 1945.

Major Franz Wilhelm Mach. Knight's Cross on 30 January 1945 while serving as commander of the 1st Battalion of the Kuban Cossack Cavalry Regiment 4. *Major* Mach commanded this battalion from mid-1943 to May 1945.

Rittmeister Günther Amelung. Knight's Cross on 15 January 1943 while serving as a *Leutnant* d.R. with the 5th company of Fast Battalion 123.
Rittmeister Amelung became acting commander of the 1st Company of Reconnaissance Battalion 55 and was killed in action in Croatia on 29 March 1944.

Rittmeister Kay Langfeldt. Knight's Cross on 18 May 1943 while serving as acting troop commander in Bicycle Battalion 30 with the rank of *Oberleutnant.*
Rittmeister Langfeldt was commander of the 2nd Battalion of the Kuban Cossack Cavalry Regiment 3 from September 1943 to May 1945.

Rittmeister Hans Jürgen Schreiber. Knight's Cross on 3 January 1943 while serving as acting commander of the 4th Company of the Division Reconnaissance Battalion 22 with the rank of *Oberleutnant.*
Rittmeister Schreiber was the commander of the 1st Battalion of the Siberian Cossack Cavalry Regiment 2 from October 1943 to April 1944. The photograph was taken while he was a *Major* (*Rittmeister* Schreiber was promoted to *Major* after his service with the Cossacks).

The Uniforms and Emblems of the Cossacks in the German Armed Forces (*Wehrmacht*)

For the most part the Cossacks wore the uniforms and rank badges of the German Army, meaning the standard tunic with collar patches (enlisted men, NCOs and officers), shoulder straps and rank badges like the other army units. Service colors were the gold-yellow of the cavalry, the bright red of the artillery, the pale yellow of the signals corps, and the black of the combat engineers (*Pioniere*). The red collar patch with crossed silver lances was outlined in green for enlisted men and non-commissioned officers and in white or silver for officers. These collar patches were introduced for Cossacks in December 1942. Not until mid-1944 was it made mandatory for Cossacks to wear the collar patches and rank badges of the German Army. In practice, however, it appears that the Cossacks had begun wearing the same badges as their German comrades prior to this date. Cossack generals wore the same collar patches as German generals. Enlisted men and NCOs wore the army belt, officers the standard brown officer's belt. Some Cossacks, however, wore the Russian belt with the German uniform. The *shashka*, the Cossack saber with smooth grip and black leather sheath, was frequently worn. With the German uniform the saber was slung from a cross belt, with the *Wehrmacht* belt fastened over it. German Army field gray breeches were generally worn, although Russian breeches were sometimes seen. The Don Cossacks mainly wore dark blue riding breeches, while some Siberian Cossacks wore blue-gray *Luftwaffe* breeches. Whenever possible, colored stripes were worn on the outer seam of the riding breeches. These stripes were sometimes worn on long trousers, though infrequently. The stripes were red for Kuban and Don Cossacks, yellow for Siberian Cossacks and blue for Terek Cossacks. The stripes of the Terek Cossacks were trimmed with black on both sides. The stripes were supposed to be five centimeters in width, however the stripes worn by the Don Cossacks were only 2.5 centimeters wide. A silver braid on each side of the stripe was prescribed for officers, but this was usually not worn. Often no clear lines were apparent in the uniforms worn by the Cossacks. Whatever was available was used. Items of captured uniforms, traditional uniforms, and shoulder straps from the former czarist army combined to give the Cossacks a unique and unpredictable appearance. Even when an attempt at standardization was made within a regiment, it rarely succeeded beyond the troop level.

The first official emblem for the Cossack units (including the Platov Cossack Regiment) was created in August 1942, initially for the security units and guard personnel. All badges worn prior to this were unofficial and for the most part procured privately. The national emblem introduced in 1942 was not worn by the 1st Cossack Division or the XV Cossack Cavalry Corps. Instead they wore the emblem of the German Army. In many other units the special Cossack emblem was not exchanged for that of the German Army until 1943. The remaining badges (shoulder straps) were worn by the Cossacks on the formation of the 1st Cossack Division. Directive No. 8000/42 applied to the following groups:

a) Members of the Turkish peoples and Cossacks, which includes:
    1. Turkish battalions, including Turkish construction battalions, etc.
    2. Cossack units
    3. Crimean Tatars
b) Domestic Units (security units) of local volunteers or released prisoners of war, which operate in the operations zone to guard their homes against straggling elements of the Russian Army, bandits and Bolshevik insurgents. These include: the Estonian, Latvian. Lithuanian, Finnish, White Russian, Ukrainian and Ethnic German security units and formations that are deployed in the operations zone.

c) Protection Units (Order Service) in the operations zone.

These include protection units formed from local volunteers or released prisoners of war in the occupied eastern regions for policing or guard purposes which are deployed as units or individually in the operations zone. Condition is, that they are principally active in the order service, not occasionally or temporarily. Under this fall:

The "Auxiliary Guard Sections" with Army Groups A and B

The "Order Service" with Army Group Center

The "Auxiliary Guard Sections" and the "Resident Combat Units" with Army Group North

d) The local volunteers and released prisoners of war that have joined the forces permanently as auxiliaries.

e) Local residents who have been drafted temporarily for special work (general labor, road work, snow clearing, position building, etc.)

f) Prisoners of war who have been drafted to work (as under e).

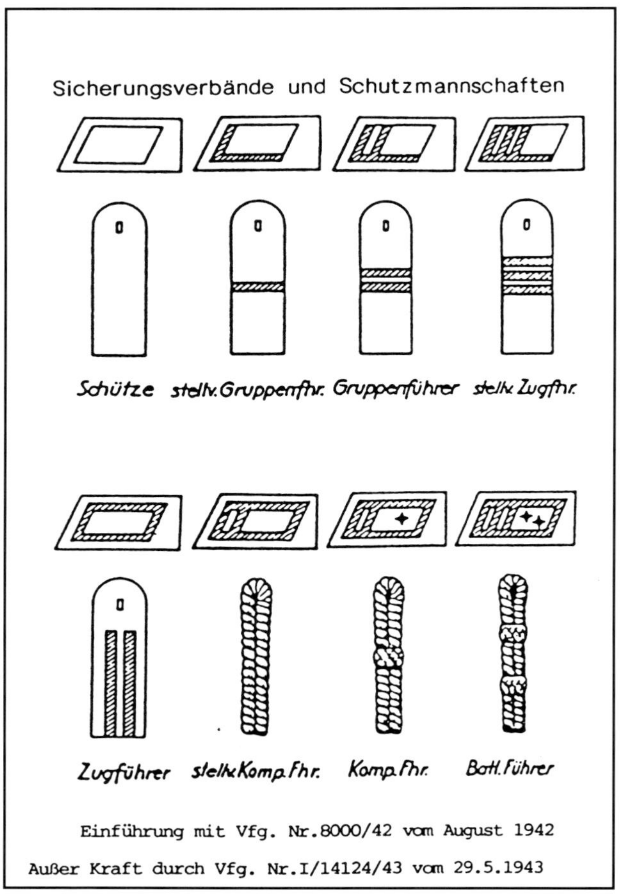

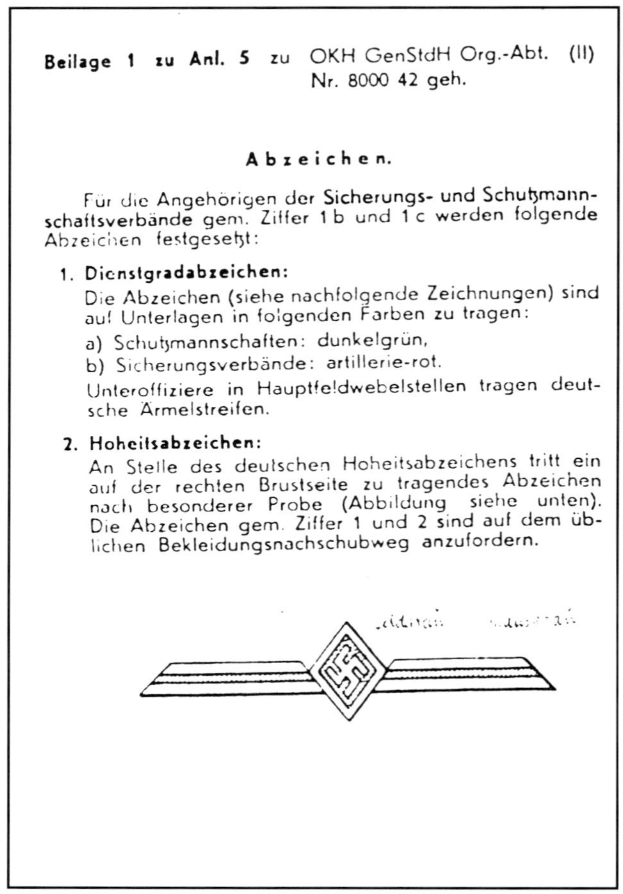

Beilage 1 zu Anl. 5 zu OKH GenStdH Org.-Abt. (II) Nr. 8000 42 geh.

Abzeichen.

Für die Angehörigen der Sicherungs- und Schutzmannschaftsverbände gem. Ziffer 1 b und 1 c werden folgende Abzeichen festgesetzt:

1. **Dienstgradabzeichen:**
   Die Abzeichen (siehe nachfolgende Zeichnungen) sind auf Unterlagen in folgenden Farben zu tragen:
   a) Schutzmannschaften: dunkelgrün,
   b) Sicherungsverbände: artillerie-rot.
   Unteroffiziere in Hauptfeldwebelstellen tragen deutsche Ärmelstreifen.

2. **Hoheitsabzeichen:**
   An Stelle des deutschen Hoheitsabzeichens tritt ein auf der rechten Brustseite zu tragendes Abzeichen nach besonderer Probe (Abbildung siehe unten).
   Die Abzeichen gem. Ziffer 1 und 2 sind auf dem üblichen Bekleidungsnachschubweg anzufordern.

Directive No. 8000/42 of August 1942.

Rank Badges of the Platov Cossack Regiment

Enlisted men and non-commissioned officers:

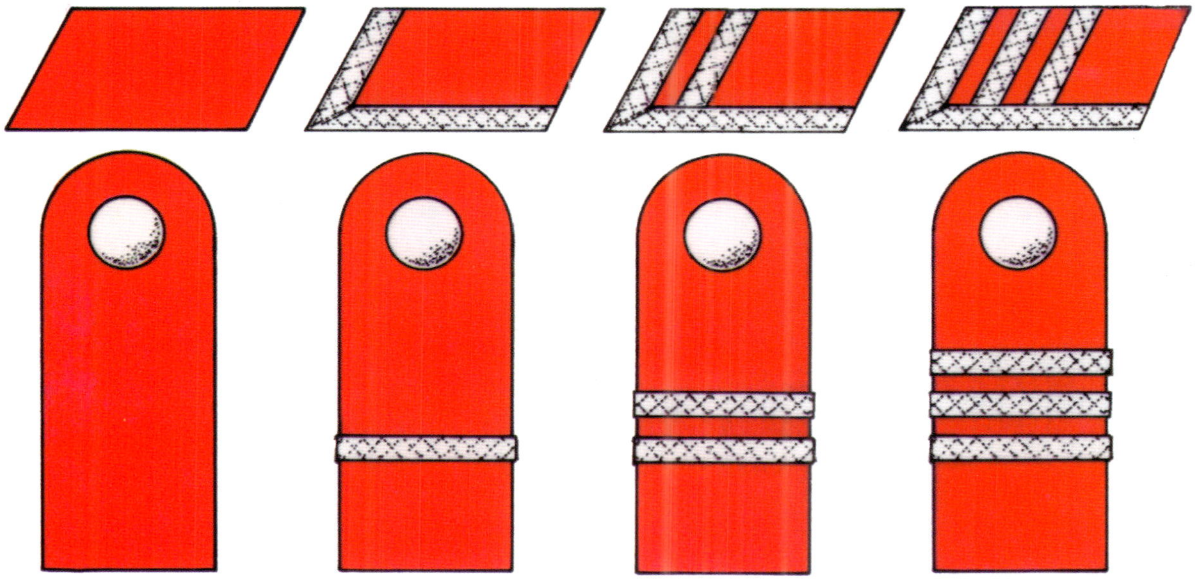

Rifleman/Trooper — Acting Squad Leader — Squad Leader — Acting Platoon Commander

The shoulder straps and collar patches for enlisted men and non-commissioned officer were red with silver braid according to rank.

Officers:

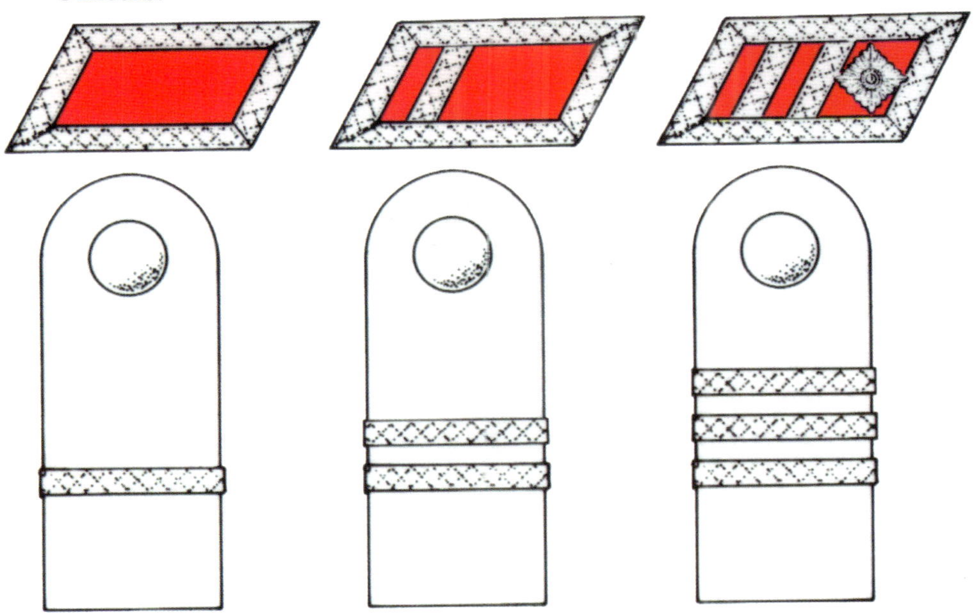

Platoon commander — Acting troop commander — Troop commander

These collar patches and shoulder straps had silver braiding and stars. They were prescribed in an order dated 13 June 1942 and introduced by the regiment. The shoulder straps for officers were white with silver braid according to rank.

On 17 June 1943 the Platov Cossack Regiment formed the 2nd Battalion of the 2nd Cossack Light Cavalry Regiment (from 24 August 1943 the 2nd Siberian Cossack Cavalry Regiment).

Enlisted men and non-commissioned officers:

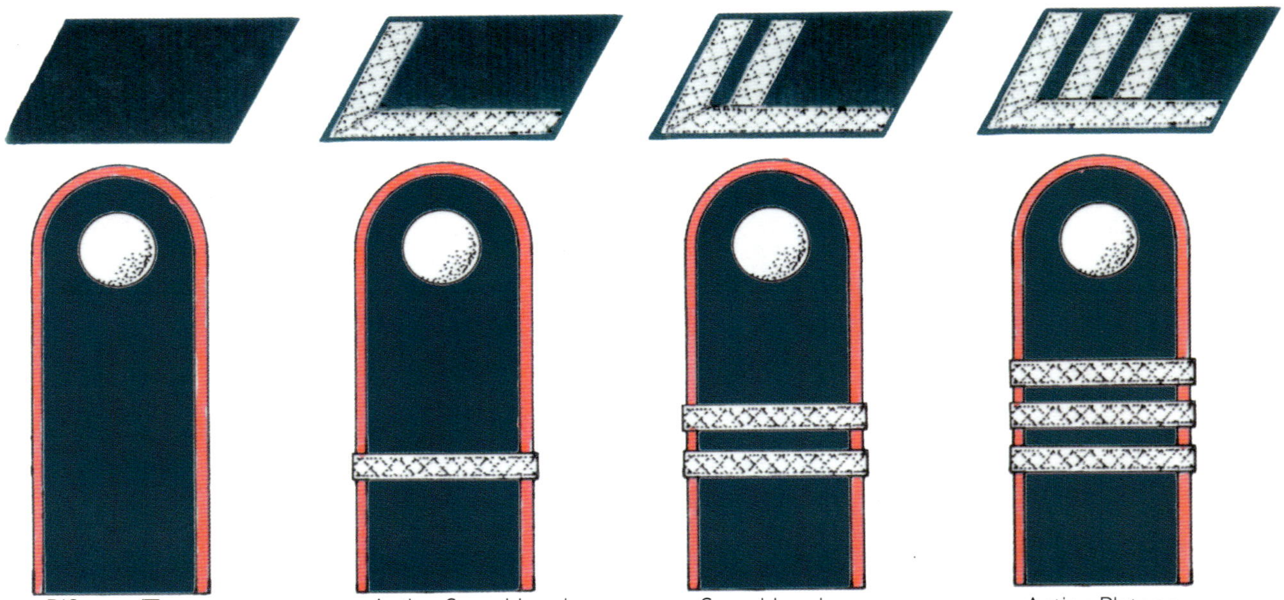

Rifleman/Trooper — Acting Squad Leader — Squad Leader — Acting Platoon Commander

An order dated 11 November 1942 changed and expanded the rank badges. The shoulder straps were now green and outlined in red. The color of the collar patches was also changed to green.

Officers:

From left to right: platoon commander, acting troop commander, troop commander, battalion commander

The silver shoulder cord for ranks from deputy troop leader up had a braided gold slide. The new rank badges had been introduced by the secret "Directive Concerning Domestic Units in the East" dated August 1942. A directive issued on 11 November 1942 required specified one braid and two stars on the shoulder straps of battalion commanders. As per the General Army Dispatch of 21 December 1942, the collar patches were replaced by special patches (crossed lances).

Signal No. 12, 2nd June issue, Page 10: Volunteers of the Russian Liberation Army from the Platov Cossack Regiment on parade to receive promotions. Propaganda Service photograph; correspondent Knödler.

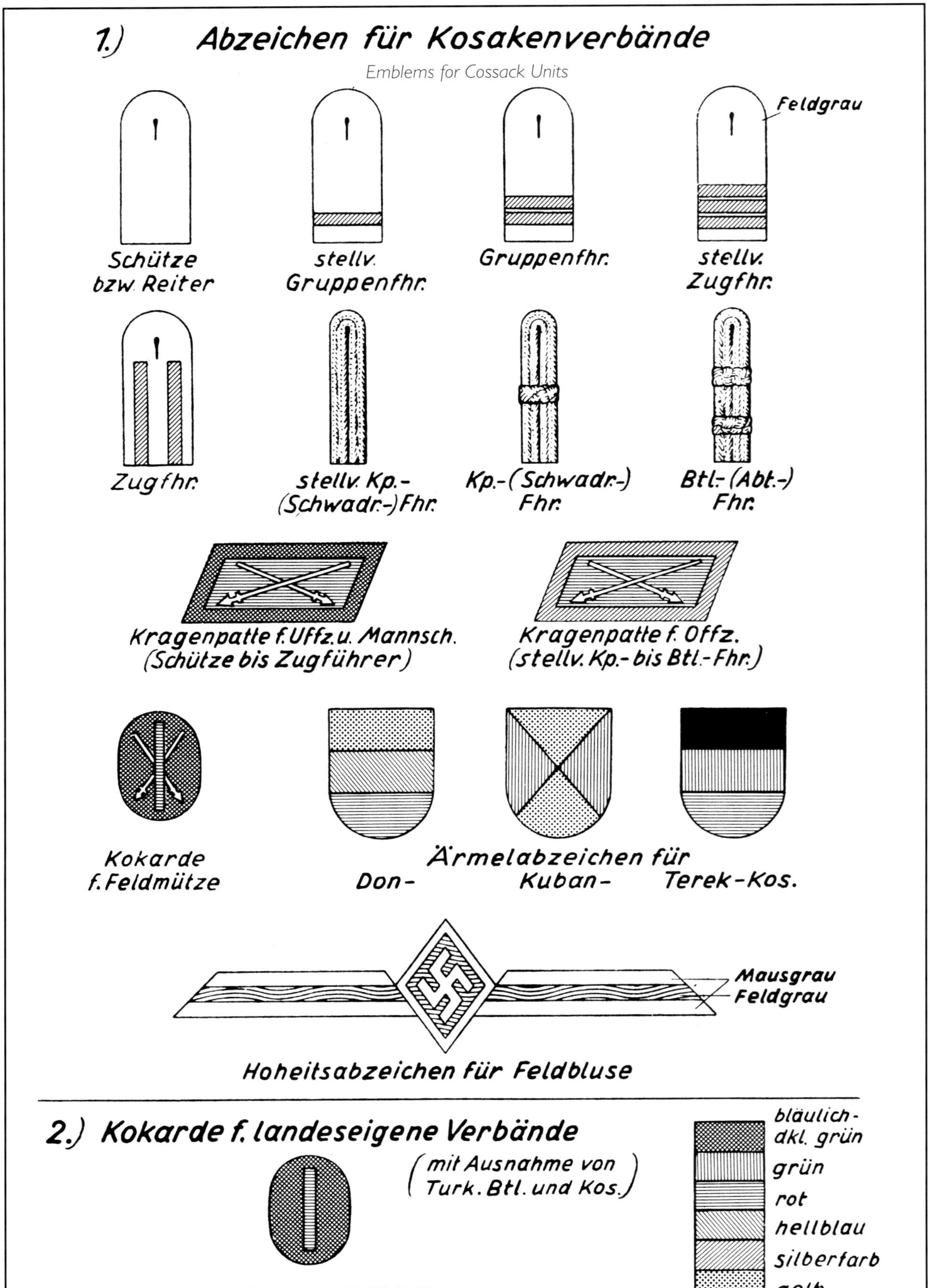

Allgemeine Heeresmitteilungen vom 21.12.1942.

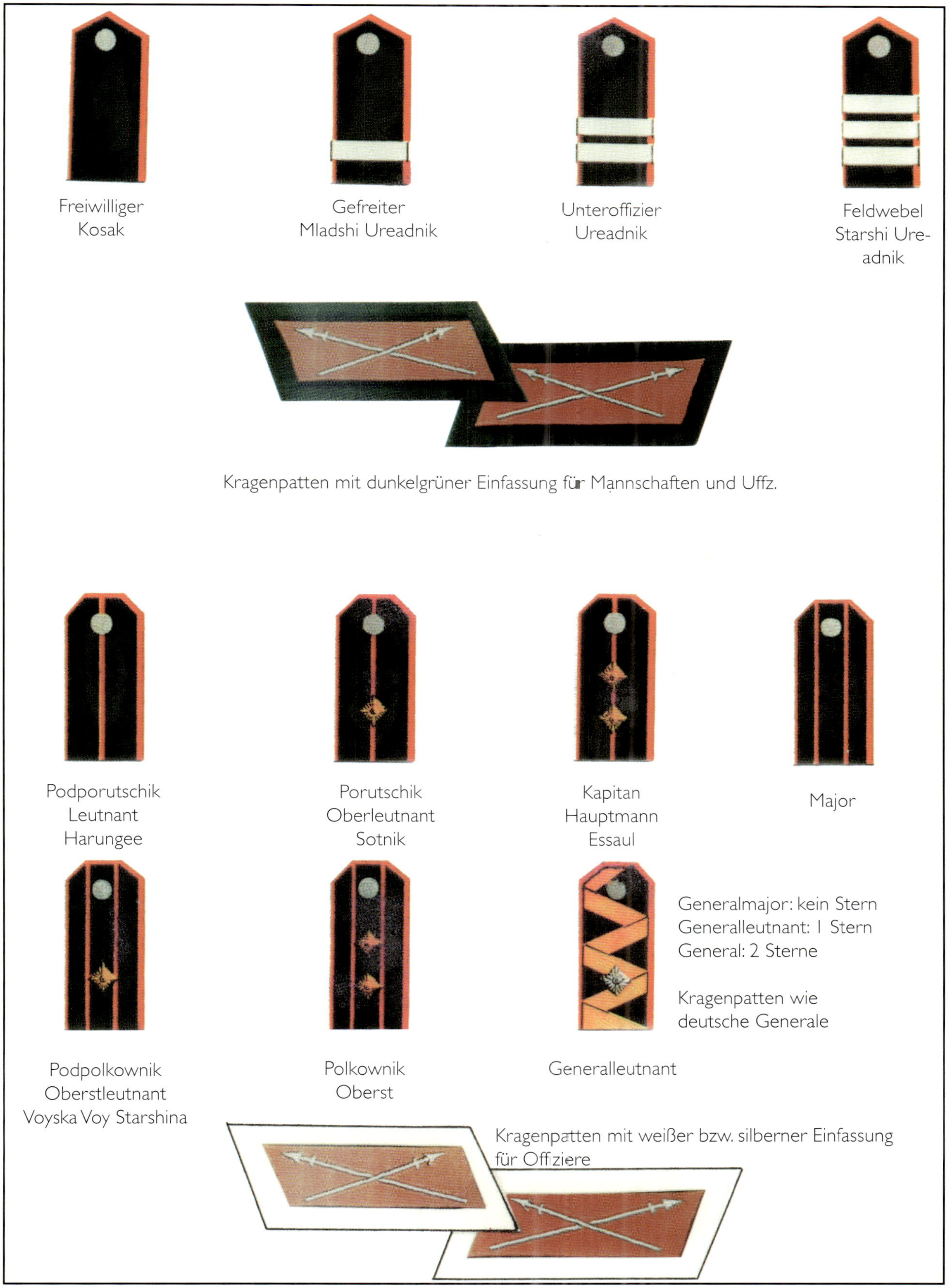

Shoulder straps and collar patches worn by Cossacks (from Signal Special Eastern Issue, December 1943). The various ranks were given in the German, Russian, and Cossack languages.

Cossack with the national emblem as per Directive No. 8000/42 and the General Army Dispatch of 21 December 1942.

Collar Patches

Two Cossack non-commissioned officers with outlined dark green collar patches and silver or white crossed lances on a red background. The Cossack on the left wears Cossack shoulder straps, while the soldier on the right wears German shoulder straps.

Collar patch for enlisted men and non-commissioned officers as per the army directive of 21 December 1942 (woven version).

German personnel attached to Cossack units also wore the Cossack collar patches.

Oberst Kononov with the silver-outlined collar patches worn by officers.

Woven version of the collar patch for Cossack officers.

The stitched version of the collar patch for Cossack officers. This collar patch was made by a unit tailoring section. The background is red cloth. The outline consists of aluminum-color NCO braid which was sewed on. The lances were made with a sewing machine.

The officer's collar patch was also made without lances, consisting of a silver outline around a red field. The cavalryman illustrated here is wearing such patches.

Shoulder Straps

Produced from both dark green and field gray cloth. There were numerous variations in the color and width of the braids.

From mid-1944 the Cossacks were officially required to wear German rank badges; even before this, however, most units had been issued German rank badges.

Rifleman, Trooper, Volunteer

Gefreiter

Unteroffizier

A Cossack Gefreiter of the Kuban Cossack Cavalry regiment 3.

A Cossack Feldwebel/Wachtmeister with the prescribed shoulcer straps.

Unteroffizier

Feldwebel/Wachtmeister

Cossack Unteroffizier of the Kuban Cossack Cavalry Regiment 3 with German shoulder straps and collar patches.

Leutnant

Oberleutnant

Shoulder strap of a *Rittmeister* (cavalry major). The light blue trim suggests that it was worn by a Terek Cossack. The shoulder strap is underlaid in black and has a tongue. The braid is silver in color, while the stars are gold-plated.

Major

Generalmajor

Battle Dress Tunics

Battle dress tunic worn by a Cossack Wachtmeister (technical sergeant). On the jacket are collar patches and shoulder straps as prescribed in 1942. On the upper right sleeve is the sleeve badge of the Don Cossacks (published in the General Army Dispatches of 21 Dec. 1942). The red trim on the button row and the buttons on the cuffs suggest a strong Czarist Army influence. The wearer obviously had this tunic privately made. This style of tunic was introduced roughly in mid-1942. The red collar patches and shoulder straps for enlisted men and non-commissioned officers were worn by the men of the Platov Cossack Regiment from about mid-1942 (exception: German personnel attached to the regiment). The Platov Cossack Regiment was formed in 1942. When the 1st Cossack Division was formed in Mielau in 1943, elements of this regiment formed the Siberian Cossack Cavalry Regiment 2.
The photograph on the right shows the same tunic worn with the shashka. The saber was slung from a cross belt, which was worn under the waist belt.

Feldbluse 36 tunic worn by a Hauptwachtmeister (Spieß, or top sergeant, denoted by the two stripes on the sleeves) of the Kuban Cossack Cavalry Regiment 4 with standard collar patches and German cavalry shoulder straps trimmed in yellow.

Battle dress tunic worn by a Cossack Unteroffizier. On the upper right sleeve is the oval sleeve badge of a division or corps headquarters. The Cossack collar patches are very simply made. The white crossed lances have been stitched on the red background. See details above.

Tropical battle dress tunic worn by a *Major* of the Siberian Cossacks.

In the Siberian Cossack Cavalry Regiment 2 of the 1st Cossack Division, the sleeve badge was worn on the upper right sleeve. Here it appears on the left. In the top buttonhole is the ribbon for the "Medal for the Winter Battle in the East". The following ribbons appear on the bar (from left to right):
Cross of St. George (Russian)
Bravery Decoration for Members of the Eastern Peoples 2nd Class in Gold with Swords (in this case awarded twice)
Bravery Decoration for Members of the Eastern Peoples 2nd Class in Silver with Swords
On the collar are the tabs for enlisted men and non-commissioned officers. See close-up above.

Battle dress tunic of an acting platoon commander or a technical sergeant of the Terek Cossacks. This garment is a modified blouse. The production of blouses was halted at the beginning of the war. A directive issued on 21 March 1940 (HM 40, No. 427) directed that members of the Replacement Army were to wear the blouse while on duty after the necessary modifications. This affected the blouse, which was no longer suitable for dress, parade or social dress. The modified blouse was worn by the enlisted men of the Replacement Army and by units of the Eastern Troops. The blouse illustrated here has a field gray collar and field gray cuffs each with two buttons. On the collar are the standard collar patches and around the collar the field gray braid for non-commissioned officers. The shoulder straps are blue and have three stripes of field gray braid.

On the upper right sleeve is the hand-made emblem of the Terek Cossacks. In the second buttonhole is the ribbon of the Bravery or Meritorious Service Medal, 2nd Class in Silver, for Members of the Eastern Peoples. It is not known in which unit this modified blouse was worn. The arm shield was worn on the left upper sleeve by members of the Terek Cossack Cavalry Regiment 6 of the 1st Cossack Division. See close-up photograph above.

The sleeve badge was 60 mm high and 49 mm wide. The underlay consisted of black material similar to felt and was surrounded by yellow cord. The death's head was pressed metal and sewed in place. Originally (as may be seen), the death's head was blackened.

The rank badges sewed onto the collar trim consist of silver-colored braid 9 mm in width. The trim on the shoulder straps and the color of the collar patches is light green.

Battle dress tunic of Cossack Police Troop 7. The tunic is the same as those worn by the German police. On the upper left sleeve is the national emblem of the police. Sewed on beneath it is the sleeve badge for members of Cossack Police Troop 7. The rank badges of an acting platoon commander (Wachtmeister) have been sewn onto the shoulder straps and collar patches.

It is not known whether this troop carried out order duties under the command of a police unit or the military police of the German Army. It is known that Cossack military police were attached to the Domanov Corps in Northern Italy. In the second buttonhole is the ribbon of the "Medal for the Winter Battle in the East 1941-42". On the small bar is the ribbon of the Bravery Decoration 2nd Class in Silver for Members of the Eastern Peoples. See close-up photographs above.

In the second buttonhole is the ribbon of the Bravery and Meritorious Service Decoration, 2nd Class in Silver, for Members of the Eastern Peoples. On the box-pleat of the left breast pocket are two eyes for a pin decoration, most likely the Iron Cross, First Class. The small bar bears the ribbons of the War Merit Cross, Second Class with Swords, the Medal for the Winter Battle in the East 1941-42, and the Defense of Germany Honor Badge. The owner sewed the ribbon of the Romanian decoration The Commemorative Medal for the Struggle against Communism next to the bar. This was done after the war, as the decoration was not usually worn this way. The medal was created by King Michael I of Romania on 1 April 1942. The tunic has plain shoulder straps. The button row has five buttons (this was changed to six buttons on 25 May 1941 by Directive HM 41, No. 558). The collar patches are made of machine-sewn pale gray yarn, a practice which was introduced in 1943.

Tunic of a Cavalry *Leutnant*, a German attached to the Kuban Cossacks. On the left upper sleeve is the sleeve badge of the Kuban Cossacks. Members of the Kuban Cossack Cavalry Regiment 3 of the 1st Cossack Division wore the arm shield on the left.

Cossack of an unidentified unit. On the upper left sleeve is a death's head on a diamond-shaped background with piping. There are no rank badges or national emblems visible on the uniform.

Feldbluse 36 tunic of an Oberwachtmeister (master sergeant) of the Division Signals Battalion 55 of the 1st Cossack Division. Collar patches and shoulder straps are the lemon-yellow color of the signals troops. The national emblem was removed after the war. Because of a shortage of sleeve badges for the division units of the 1st Cossack Division (colors: yellow, red, blue), the earlier sleeve badge of the Don Cossacks (yellow, blue, red) was used at first. The legend "DON" was either resewn or removed. The vertical yellow stripe identifies the Division Signals Battalion 55.

Trouser Stripes

The members of division units (medical battalion, veterinary company, division supply, etc.) wore narrow red stripes on their trousers similar to those worn by the Kuban regiments. The division reconnaissance battalion did not wear trouser stripes.

The Oberwachtmeister depicted here (left in photograph) wears the Anti-Partisan Badge on the left side of his tunic. On his riding breeches he wears the blue stripe, 5 cm wide and trimmed in black, of the Terek Cossack Cavalry Regiment 6.

Left: Officers of Siberian Cossack Cavalry Regiment 2. On their riding breeches may be seen the five-centimeter-wide yellow stripes. Those worn by the Don Cossacks were red, while those worn by the Terek Cossacks were blue lined with black. Right: Croatia, summer 1944. Two Cossack *Rittmeister* and troop commanders of the Don Cossack Cavalry Regiment 5. The wide red stripes may be seen on their riding breeches.

Uniform Badges of the Guard Troop

Leutnant Boychevsky joined the 1st Cossack Division as acting commander of the Guard Troop in 1943. He was later promoted to *Oberleutnant* and *Rittmeister*. The Guard Troop was attached to the headquarters commander (1st Cossack Division) and later the headquarters commander of the XV Cossack Cavalry Corps. The Guard Troop, also called *Konvoy*, was supposed to be expanded into the Corps Guard Battalion with four troops, however this plan could not be realized before the end of the war.

Rittmeister Boychevsky with members of the Guard Troop.

Cossack *Leutnant* Boychevsky, commander of the Guard Troop of the 1st Cossack Division. The bulava is worn as a shield on his upper right sleeve. On the lower sleeve is a chevron in broad golden braid. The Guard Troop commander wore Czarist shoulder straps, enlisted men and non-commissioned officers red shoulder straps. In keeping with his rank, gold-colored braid was sewed across the shoulder straps. The collar braid for officers was also gold in color. (See members of the Guard Troop in the paintings of Olaf Jordan.)

Oberleutnant (later *Rittmeister*) Alexei Boychevsky (the rank of *Rittmeister* is not visible in this photograph) wearing the cherkesska of the Guard Troop. The braid chevron is visible on the left sleeve.

The Czarist shoulder strap of a Harungee (Lieutenant). These shoulder straps could be seen on *Rittmeister* Boychevsky's cherkesska and tunic.

The cherkesska of the former commander of the Guard Troop of the XV Cossack Cavalry Corps, *Rittmeister* Boychevsky (photographed in the Military Museum in Rastatt). On the left upper sleeve of the cherkesska is the sleeve badge of the Kuban Cossacks and on the upper right sleeve the sleeve badge of the Guard Troop or Division Headquarters (not visible here). The sleeve badge of the Kuban Cossacks was added at a later date. In contemporary photographs of *Rittmeister* Boychevsky only the emblem of the Guard Troop is seen on his cherkesska.

Soldiers of the Guard Troop. The chevron has also been applied to their coats.

Rittmeister Boychevsky (center) with a Cossack officer of the Guard Troop (right) and a German officer.

Tunic of a squad leader or Unteroffizier of the Guard Troop of the 1st Cossack Division. The dark green shoulder straps are timed in red. The braid on the shoulder straps and lower sleeve are gold in color. The crossed lances have been stitched onto the collar patches.

Tunic of a squad leader or Unteroffizier of the Guard Troop of the 1st Cossack Division, later XV Cossack Cavalry Corps. The gold braid on the collar, on the shoulder straps and the lower sleeves is 7 mm wide. Collar patches: 73 mm long, 33 mm wide. Here the lances are simple in form, consisting of silver stripes. The double chevron was 145 mm high and 145 mm wide at the bottom.

The members of the Guard Troop wore a double chevron on their battle dress tunics, overcoats and *cherkesskas*. It is not known for certain whether all members of the Guard Troop wore the double chevron or just deserving Cossacks who had been decorated with it. It is to be assumed that the chevron had its origins in a tradition from the days of the Czars.

Moscow, 1913. The Imperial couple during celebrations marking the 300th anniversary of the Romanov dynasty. The Czar's son Alexey is being carried by one of the Czar's bodyguards. On the left is the Czarina Alexandra and in the center Nicholas II. Chevrons may be seen on the supper sleeve of the bodyguard's cherkesska. This chevron is open at the top. The chevrons worn by the Cossack of the Guard Troop of the 1st Cossack Division and the XV Cossack Cavalry Corps were open at the bottom. It is impossible to say whether there was any direct connection.

The *Cherkesska*

As well as being the parade uniform of the guard troop, the *cherkesska* was also the dress uniform of the Cossacks. The *cherkesska* was a boot-length coat, black, field gray or dark blue, worn by the Kuban and Terek Cossacks. In the 1st Cossack Division and XV Cossack Cavalry Corps it was worn by the members of the Guard Troop and the Song and Dance Choir. This parade uniform was designed as follows: on each side of the *cherkesska*, breast-high, was a row of cartridge pouches. The individual elements were made of a more or less ornate material. The Cossack portraits done by Olaf Jordan depict members of the Guard Troop, and German rifle bullets may be seen in their cartridge pouches.

A Cossack NCO of the Kuban Cossacks.

Cossacks of the Guard Troop of the 1st Cossack Division in their cherkesskas.

Cossacks take advantage of a rest stop to do a little dancing. Note the red bashlyk on the back of the dancer in the center of the photograph.

A German officer attached to a Cossack unit. On his head is a white papachka. His cherkesska is quite ornate, with silver braid on the cuffs, the button row and the V-neck. The white bashlyk is worn under the pojas, to which is attached a beautiful dagger (kindshal).

General Pannwitz and *Oberst* von Bosse, both wearing the cherkesska.

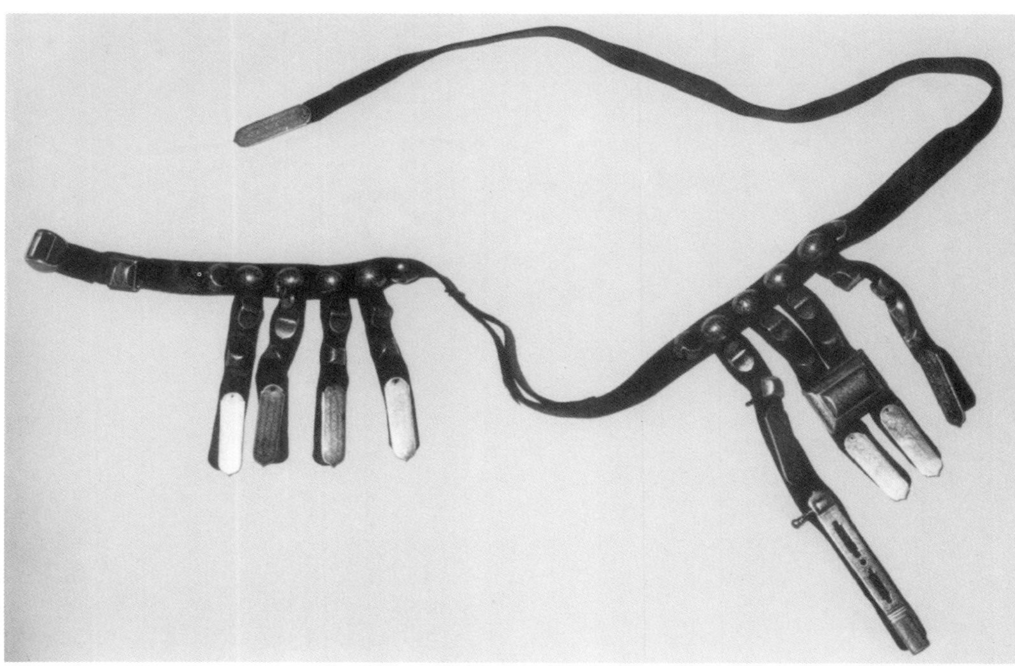

The silver-trimmed leather belt, or pojas, worn with the cherkesska. When the belt was worn, the metal- or bone-trimmed leather straps lay on the thigh. Their likely purpose was to prevent the wearer from being struck by the saber.

Generalleutnant Helmuth von Pannwitz. Beneath his cherkesska he wears a red beshmet trimmed with silver braid. The cartridge holders are plainly visible. On his head is a lambskin papachka. Around his neck is a long revolver cord, something worn only by him. The Cossacks (including officers) of the 1st Cossack Division and XV Cossack Cavalry Corps did not carry revolvers, however the expression "Revolver Cord", which had its origins in the days of the Czar, was retained for tradition's sake.

The *cherkesska* was held together by the *pojas*, a narrow belt trimmed with silver or finely carved ivory or bone. Attached to the belt was the *kindshal*, the long Circassian dagger. Attached loosely around the neck, and worn on the back, was the *bashlyk* (a hood which was pulled over the head in cold weather and which could be wrapped around the neck). Under the *cherkesska* the Cossack wore the *beshmet*, a red or black shirt made of silk or cotton with a standing collar, over the trousers. The *beshmet* had no buttons, instead it was closed using concealed hooks and eyes.

An officer's cherkesska. The shoulder straps are missing (they were removed after the war). On his head the officer wears a papachka.

The *Bashlyk*

The *bashlyk* was a large hood with two long sleeve-like ends. It was usually worn as a hood over the head or as a cape on the back. The Cossacks of Cossack Battalion 600 made their own *bashlyks*, consequently there were variations in color. The members of Don Cossack Cavalry Regiment 5 and the Guard Troop wore only the red *bashlyk* as provided by the supply section. In most cases the *bashlyk* had colored trim: Kuban Cossacks red, Siberian and Terek Cossacks blue, Don Cossacks and the Guard Troop black. The word *bashlyk* comes from the Turk and its approximate meaning is "What is above."

Bashlyk of the Don Cossacks or the Guard Troop.

Field gray bashlyk with red trim and tassel. This bashlyk was delivered from the clothing stores and issued to the Kuban Cossacks. The manufacturer's label (bottom photo, seam above the stamp) has been removed. The stamp, which is still visible, reads: 3/ABT. 3, which means, 3rd Troop, Kuban Cossack Cavalry Regiment 3.

Mielau, 1943. The honor guard conducts saber drills in front of the guardhouse. The guard commander (on the right of the photograph) wears a light-colored (white?) bashlyk on his back.

The *Burka*

The *burka* was worn on and off duty in bad weather or cold. It was a stiff cloak of pressed camel hair, which reached almost to the ankles of a standing man. At the front, the garment could be closed at the throat by a clasp or cord. When the wearer was on horseback, this piece of Cossack clothing covered the horse from the saddle to the croup and thus shielded both rider and mount from the cold and wet.

Oberst Kononov wearing the full-length burka.

This photograph illustrates how the burka protected the horse and rider.

Cossack Headgear

Generally, Cossack headgear consisted of a fur cap, of which there were two basic types, the *kubanka* and the *papachka*. The *kubanka* was a short round fur cap which was rather wider at the top. It was worn by the Kuban and Terek Cossacks. The other, the *papachka*, was taller and rather narrower at the top (conical). It was worn by the Don and Siberian Cossacks. There were exceptions, however: members of the Don Cossack Cavalry Regiments 1 and 5 and of Siberian Cossack Cavalry Regiment 2 sometimes also wore the *kubanka*. Affixed to the front of the fur caps were the matte silver German emblems: the national emblem and the black-white-red cockade in a wreath of oak leaves. These emblems were not universal, however. Cockades in the colors of the relevant Cossack army were sometimes worn instead of the German emblems, though this was rare. The German emblems appeared in both cloth and stitched forms and were sewn onto the cap.

The fur caps were made of black fleece and only the Siberian Cossacks wore white *papachkas*. This rule was not strictly adhered to, however, and it was possible to see white *kubankas* with red, cornflower blue and yellow tops. The Siberian Cossacks also wore black *kubankas* with yellow tops. The top usually matched the color of the affected Cossack regiment: red for Don and Kuban, cornflower blue for Terek, and yellow for Siberian. It should be noted, however, that field gray, black and white tops were also worn. These fur caps were made of sheepskin, while those of the officers were made of one of two types lambskin, *krimmer*, from Crimean lambs, or *karakul*, from a breed of sheep from the Parmir region.

On the caps worn by all ranks there was a cross of silver or gray braid on the cloth top. Sometimes silver stripe or black cord was simply sewed into the form of a cross. The *papachkas* worn by the Don Cossacks were an exception, as there was no cross on their red tops. The cross of silver braid appeared only on some privately-made *papachkas* worn by officers. At the end of 1944 a tobacco factory in Lichtenfels near Coburg sent the 1st Cossack Division a shipment of *papachkas*. They had a red cloth top, but no braid or national emblem, and were made of goatskin. Rank badges for officers were to be of silver striping running around the outer edge of the top around the cap as follows:

Leutnant:	1 stripe
Oberleutnant:	2 stripes
Hauptmann (Rittmeister):	3 stripes
Major:	1 braid and 1 stripe
Oberstleutnant:	1 braid and 2 stripes
Oberst:	1 braid and 3 stripes

It must be stated that, while these edgings were seen, the multiple stripes described above were not, even though the wearer was of high rank. The title of the directive concerning the stripes is now known.

In action Cossacks usually wore a steel helmet, less frequently a garrison cap. Some Cossacks wore the fur cap in action, even though the wearing of this headgear in combat was forbidden. In the rear area and in quarters, however, personnel could choose to wear the *papachka* or *kubanka*.

One unique feature which should be mentioned here is the wearing of a forelock, mainly by young Cossacks. This long lock of hear on the forehead was worn outside the fur cap, giving the Cossack a rather wild appearance. This forelock was called *chub* by the Don Cossacks and *cholka* by the Kuban Cossacks.

A Cossack officer wearing the steel helmet.

The various types of headgear may be seen in this photograph. The two Cossack Wachtmeister in the left and right foreground are wearing the kubanka, while the one in the center wears a steel helmet. In the background are Cossacks wearing the forage cap and Feldmütze 43 garrison cap.

Page 60: Officers and Wachtmeister of Cossack Battalion 600, which later became the Don Cossack Cavalry Regiment 5. The photograph was taken in Mogilev in December 1942. Note the various types of headwear (kubankas and papachkas). It is impossible to say whether the cockades are the official version or the earlier non-official badge.

Yugoslavia, 1944. A Cossack wearing the Feldmütze 38 garrison cap.

Mielau, 1943. Cossack officer wearing the Feldmütze 43 field cap.

Mielau, about mid-1943. The soldier on the left is wearing a kubanka. The officers wear Soviet peaked caps, five of them with an unidentified oval cockade. The Unteroffizier in the center has the German emblem on his peaked cap. All of the soldiers illustrated are carrying a saber (shashka). The Unteroffizier second from the left is wearing a Soviet belt.

Feldmütze 38 garrison cap for officers. On the top seam is a silver stripe made of aluminum thread and on the front edge of the flap a red cord. The color of the cockade suggests the Don Army. The cockade is an early, unofficial version with the St. Andrew's Cross in the center.

Mogilev, early 1942. A Cossack officer of Cossack Battalion 600 wearing the Feldmütze 38. He also wears the collar patches for enlisted men and non-commissioned officers and the narrow shoulder straps of an acting troop commander. The garrison cap has the soutache chevron, whose color must have been red.

Mielau, 1943. A Cossack Wachtmeister of the Don Cossack Cavalry Regiment 5. He is wearing German shoulder straps on his German tunic with the special collar patches for Cossacks. On his head is a Soviet peaked cap with German emblems.

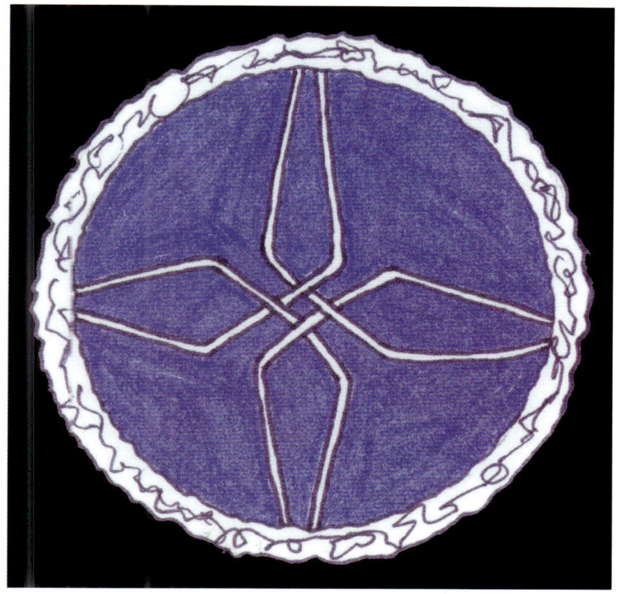

Reconstructions of several cap tops.

Croatia, late 1943. Cossacks of the 1st Battalion of the Kuban Cossack Cavalry Regiment 4 receive decorations. Not the braid cross on the officer's hat. This cross usually consisted of aluminum braid of varying widths. There were also versions in which the cross was made of silver striping and black cord.

An unidentified Cossack soldier. Note the forelock emerging from beneath his fur cap.

Black fleece kubanka with German emblems in metal. The blue cap top suggests the Terek Cossacks. On the top is a cross of silver braid.

Kubanka for members of the Kuban Cossack Cavalry Regiments 3 and 4; it was also worn by the Don Cossack Cavalry Regiments 1 and 5.

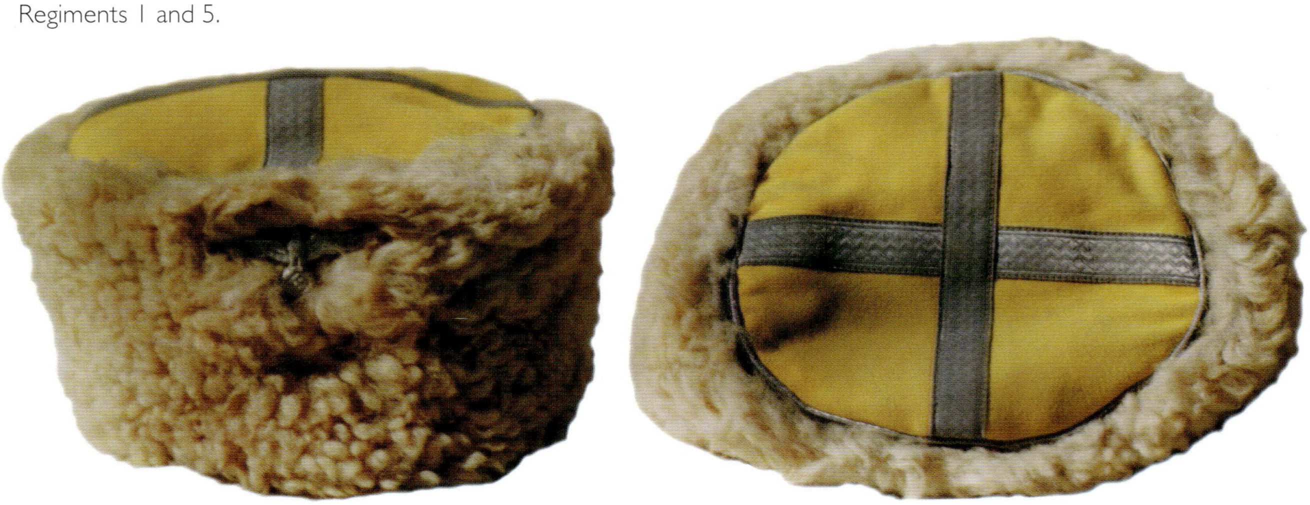

This kubanka for Siberian Cossacks was worn by an officer, as indicated by the silver trim around the cap top.

Black fleece kubanka worn by the Siberian Cossacks. The more elaborate cross on the cap top is made of silver braid. This kubanka is also rather taller than usual and somewhat conical in shape.

Russian-made kubanka of white fleece with a red top, indicating the Kuban Cossacks. It was also worn by the Don Cossacks.

Bottom view of the kubanka illustrated on the right, bearing the stamp "Clothing Stores – Cracow 1943."

The outer edge of the top of this kubanka is trimmed with braid, indicating the rank of *Leutnant*. Two rows of silver braid in the form of a cross have been sewn onto the blue cap top (Terek Cossacks).

A German officer serving with a Cossack unit wearing a kubanka.

A Cossack wearing a kubanka of light-colored fleece.

On this kubanka the cross on the top, here made of silver braid, is clearly visible.

Cossack wearing a white kubanka. It closely resembles the one illustrated on Page 65 (center).

Don Cossack wearing a papachka. On his left sleeve is the blue and red emblem of the Don Cossack Cavalry Regiment 5.

Black fleece papachka with red top as worn by the Don Cossacks. The officially-produced papachkas did not have the cross of silver braid on the top. Braid crosses only appeared on privately-made caps for officers.

Oberst Kononov (right) wearing a papachka. On the cap is the special cockade for officers of the Don Cossacks.

Privately-made papachka of goatskin with red top.

A German *Leutnant* attached to a Cossack unit wearing the white papachka of the Don Cossack Cavalry Regiment 5.

Cockades

The officers' cockades were oval with serrated edges, while those worn by the enlisted men and non-commissioned officers were oval with a smooth edge. These cockades were rarely worn. In most cases the Cossacks wore the emblem of the German Army on their headgear, while the German personnel attached to Cossack units wore the German emblem almost exclusively. In many Cossack units of the German armed forces, the old Czarist cockades were seen on *kubankas* and *papachkas*. German emblems were not worn on the *papachka*. *Papachkas* were either completely devoid of emblems or bore Cossack or Czarist cockades.

Don Cossacks (blue-red)

Terek Cossacks (black-blue)

Kuban Cossacks (black-red)

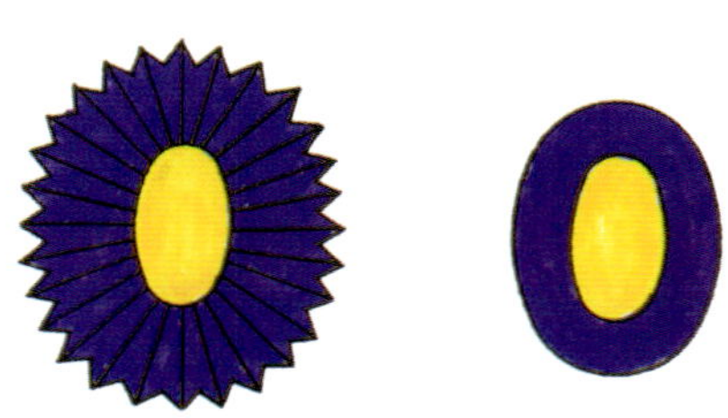

Siberian Cossacks (blue-yellow)

The front and rear of a metal cockade for officers of the ROA (Russian Liberation Army), which was similar to that of the Cossacks. No original cockade for Cossack officers could be found.

This cockade was officially introduced following the release of the General Army Dispatch of 21 December 1942.

A German *Rittmeister* attached to a unit of Don Cossacks. On his papachka is the cockade for officers of the Don Cossacks.

Cossack officer wearing the cockade illustrated above on his garrison cap.

These cockade versions for non-commissioned officers and enlisted men were made of metal, were painted in matte colors and had four holes in the edge for sewing onto the garrison or peaked cap, kubankas or papachkas. The cockade of the Don Cossacks was colored gray-blue and red, that of the Kuban Cossacks black and red, and that of the Terek Cossacks black and gray-blue.

Reconstruction of an unofficial cockade worn by the Don Cossacks. In the center on the red field is the St. Andrew's Cross. The St. Andrew's Cross was the emblem of the Czarist fleet. This cockade was worn prior to the introduction of the approved version (see Page 68).

Young Cossack of the Don Cossack Cavalry Regiment 5 wearing the cockade described above.

Unidentified cockade.

The youngest member of the Kuban Cossack Cavalry Regiment 3, Croatia, Easter 1944. The significance of the cockade on his kubanka is not known.

Czarist Cockades

Enlisted men

non-commissioned officers

officers

Other Cap Badges

Death's Head emblem of Cavalry Regiment 5, recalling the earlier Prussian 1st and 2nd Bodyguard Hussar Regiments. This emblem was worn by former members of Cavalry Regiment 5, however some Cossacks used this martial-looking emblem to decorate their kubankas.

Oberstleutnant Prince zu Salm-Horstmar as commander of Terek Cossack Cavalry Regiment 6. On his fur cap he wears the death's head of Cavalry Regiment 5.

Cossack with burka. On his kubanka is an as yet unidentified emblem.

Sleeve Badges (Arm Shields)

At the beginning of 1942 regimental commanders issued orders for cloth sleeve badges, allowing their imaginations to run wild. Those delivered through official channels were mostly woven. The first official arm shields for the Cossacks were introduced in December 1942. In 1942-43 there were sleeve badges with the name of the associated Cossack army, which was stitched into the black edging above the colored emblem. For the Don Cossacks this was blue, for the Kuban Cossacks yellow and for the Terek Cossacks green. The Terek Cossacks are known to have had a second shield with silver-gray lettering. New emblems were introduced in the autumn of 1943, first being illustrated in a special eastern edition of *Signal* in December 1943. These sleeve badges were not announced in the Army Regulations Gazette until 17 July 1944. At the same time a directive was issued stating that from then on volunteers would also wear German rank badges. Instead of the entire title, the new badges had only an abbreviation of the associated Cossack army in Cyrillic letters. For the Don Cossacks this was BA, for the Siberians NCB, for the Kuban Cossacks KB and for the Terek Cossacks TB, which meant:

BA:	*Voyska Donskoye* Don Army
NCB:	*Polk Sibirski Voina Voysky* Siberian War Regiment
KB:	*Kubanskiye Voyska* Kuban Troops
TB:	*Terskiye Voyska* Terek Troops

Wearing of arm shields in the 1st Cossack Division and XV Cossack Cavalry Corps:

Don Cossack Cavalry Regiment 1	right sleeve
Don Cossack Cavalry Regiment 5	left sleeve
Kuban Cossack Cavalry Regiment 3	right sleeve
Kuban Cossack Cavalry Regiment 4	right sleeve
Terek Cossack Cavalry Regiment 6	left sleeve
Siberian Cossack Cavalry Regiment 2	right sleeve

Emblems for the division units (Cossack Pioneer Battalion, Cossack Division Signals Battalion 55, Cossack Horse artillery Battalion 55, Veterinary Company, Division Supply, and Cossack Replacement Regiment) were introduced in the autumn of 1943. The emblems were yellow-red-blue in color, and a vertical or diagonal stripe sewed over the badge identified the various battalions:

Division Signals Battalion 55:	vertical yellow stripe, on right sleeve
Pioneer Battalion 55:	vertical black stripe, on right sleeve
1st Horse Artillery Btl. 55:	vertical red stripe, on right sleeve
2nd Horse Artillery Btl. 55:	red stripe sewed diagonally over the emblem, on left sleeve
Reconnaissance Battalion 55:	black-yellow, on right sleeve

Note concerning the coloring of emblems of the division units: because of a shortage of sleeve badges for the division units, for which the colors yellow-red-blue had been specified, the units turned to the emblem of the Don Cossacks, which was also yellow-blue-red. The emblem bore the legend "Don", which was resewn or removed. This information was provided by former members of the Artillery and Signals Battalions 55 (the Don Cossacks had no artillery or signals units of their own).

There was a special arm shield for the Guard Troop, the Trumpet Corps, the Military Police, the Dispatch Rider Platoon and the Culture and Entertainment Platoon. This badge was blue outlined in red encompassing the *bulava* (Ataman emblem) and crossed sabers. It was worn on the right sleeve of the uniform shirt or tunic.

There were also unofficial emblems. Some Cossacks wore an arm shield bearing a death's head. There were also emblem-type arm shields (red with diagonal silver or white stripes) or in the form of a white triangle.

Sleeve Badges of the Headquarters of the 1st Cossack Division

The basic color of this badge was blue with a red outline. Within it are the bulava (Ataman emblem and crossed sabers). It was designed by Special Commander (K) Timm, interpreter in the headquarters staff of the 1st Cossack Division, in 1942. The badge was first worn in Mielau in autumn 1943, however most qualified to wearers did not receive their badges until early 1944 in Croatia.

The division pope of the 1st Cossack Division wearing the badge of the division headquarters.

Sleeve Badges of the Division Units

Worn by the medical battalion, veterinary company, division supply, and the Cossack Replacement Regiment. The badge was worn on the right sleeve of the uniform.

This *Leutnant* wears the sleeve badge of the division units on his upper left sleeve. The badge was usually worn on the upper right sleeve.

Cossack Division Signals Battalion 55. Worn on right sleeve.

Cossack Pioneer Battalion 55. Worn on the right sleeve

Non-commissioned officer of the 2nd (Horse) Cossack Artillery Battalion. On the upper left sleeve is the sleeve badge with the vertical red stripe. In this battalion the proper position of this stripe was diagonally across the badge.

Badge of the 1st (Horse) Cossack Artillery Battalion 55. Worn on the right sleeve with vertical red stripe.

2nd (Horse) Cossack Artillery Battalion 55. Worn on left sleeve.

Officers and non-commissioned officers of the 2nd (Horse) Battalion, Cossack Artillery Battalion 55. Several of the men are wearing the correct style of badge, with the red cloth stripe sewn diagonally across the badge.

Sleeve badge of the Division Reconnaissance Battalion 55, introduced in early 1944.

Unteroffizier of the Division Reconnaissance Battalion 55 with the sleeve badge on the upper right sleeve of his tunic. This battalion consisted entirely of German personnel, who wore German headgear exclusively. This NCO has put on the kubanka to have his picture taken (verbal account).

Cossack Division Signals Battalion 55. One emblem with the original title and one resewn without it. The yellow stripe on the emblem on the left is wrong, as it should have been positioned vertically.

2nd (Mounted) Cossack Artillery Battalion 55

Don Cossack Arm Shields

Introduced by secret OKH directive on 15 November 1942.

1942/43

1942/43

1942/43

1942/43.

Ab Mai 1943.

1942-43 From the left: *Oberst* von Schultz, *Oberst* von Bosse and *Oberst* Kononov. The latter wears the sleeve badge of the Don Cossack Cavalry Regiment 5 on the left sleeve of his tunic.

Sleeve badge (final version) for the Don Cossack Cavalry Regiments 1 and 5, from 1943-44.

A female Cossack medic of the Don Cossack Cavalry Regiment 1 in front of her quarters with the daughter of quarters provider. The sleeve badge has been sewn on her upper right sleeve. The jacket is English battle dress.

Arm Shields of the Kuban Cossacks

Circa 1942. Colors as per Littlejohn (Foreign Legions, Vol. 4)

This version was introduced by a secret OKH directive on 15 November 1942.

Circa 1942. Colors as per H. Greehey (Adjutant's Call, No. 4/5)

1942/43.

Machine-sewn version of the badge.

Specially-produced version of the badge.

Sleeve badge for the Kuban Cossack Cavalry Regiments 3 and 4, from 1943-44 (final version).

Rittmeister Arnodt of the Kuban Cossack Cavalry Regiment 4. This regiment wore the arm shield on the right sleeve of the uniform.

Sleeve badge of the Kuban Cossacks hand-sewn onto field-gray cloth. Dimensions: 66 x 59 mm; the letters are 12 mm high. The border around the shield is 1-mm silver cord.

Rittmeister Langfeldt (right) with the arm shield of the 3rd Kuban Regiment on the left upper sleeve of his coat.

Arm Shields of the Terek Cossacks

This badge was introduced by secret OKH directive on 15 November 1942.

1942-43. Date of introduction is not known.

From 1943 following the formation of the 1st Cossack Division in Mielau.

Handmade sleeve badge of the Terek Cossacks. The diagonally-divided shield is on a field-gray background. Width 65 mm, height 75 mm.

Sleeve badge for the Terek Cossack Cavalry Regiment 6, from 1944 (final version).

Rittmeister von Bila. The Terek Cossacks wore the arm shield on the upper left sleeve of the uniform.

Mielau, 21 September 1943: Major der Reserve von Kalben (C.O. of the Terek Cossack Cavalry Regiment 6) wearing the badge with the title "TEREK" on the left sleeve of his tunic. On his breeches are blue stripes trimmed in black.

Arm Shields of the Siberian Cossacks

Two different styles of the sleeve badge for the Siberian Cossack Cavalry Regiment 2, from 1944 (final version).

This sleeve badge (printed version) was supposedly also worn by the Siberian Cossacks, although no proof of this has been discovered.

Siberian Cossack with the arm shield on the upper right sleeve of his tunic. The national emblem is reversed, as it has been sewn on with the back side facing out. He wears the white papachka favored by the Siberian Cossacks.

Cossack Wachtmeister of the Siberian Cossack Cavalry Regiment 2.

Cossack Qualification Badges

Excerpt from a report by the IVa (Division Administrator) to the Ib (2nd General Staff Officer/Supply Section) concerning the actions of the Cossack in Yugoslavia (area of operations from 28 Sept. to 24 Oct. 1943):

Qualification Badges for Cossacks:
All Cossacks who have earned qualification badges are to be issued them immediately. The required gold braid is to be obtained from the Div.Abt. IVa. Completion report to be submitted by 20 Oct. 1943.

These so-called "Cossack Qualification Badges" must have been the horizontal braid worn above the sleeve badge by the Cossacks as well as by some Cossack officers. A color painting of a Cossack officer of the Kuban Cossack Cavalry Regiment 4 by the artist Olaf Jordan shows a gold-yellow braid above the sleeve badge.

It is not known who created this qualification badge and until when it was awarded within the 1st Cossack Division or XV Cossack Cavalry Corps.

These two photographs depict Cossacks of the Kuban Cossack Cavalry Regiment 3. Visible above the arm shields is the braid of the qualification badge. These photographs were taken in Croatia, Easter of 1944.

The von Jungschulz Cavalry Regiment

At the end of August 1942 *Oberstleutnant* Jungschulz von Roebern assumed command of the Prince von Urach Cavalry Regiment, which then became the von Jungschulz Cavalry Regiment. The regiment's family tree provides the following dates:

11 May 1942 formed as Prince von Urach Cavalry Battalion
15 Aug. 1942 renamed the Prince von Urach Cavalry Regiment
30 Aug. 1942 renamed the von Jungschulz Cavalry Regiment
15 Feb. 1943 renamed Cossack Regiment 1 (v. Jungschulz)
1 June 1943 renamed 3rd Cossack Cavalry Regiment Svodno
26 June 1943 renamed 3rd Cossack Cavalry Regiment (Svodnye)
5 Aug. 1943 renamed Kuban Cossack Cavalry Regiment 3

Oberstleutnant Jungschulz von Roebern remained the regimental commander until the end of January 1944.

Portrait of a troop commander. He wears a death's head emblem on his garrison cap and a death's head badge on his upper left sleeve. Note the absence of the national emblem and collar patches from his tunic.

Major, later *Oberstleutnant*, Werner Jungschulz von Roebern, first commander of the Kuban Cossack Cavalry Regiment 3. On his kubanka is the German national emblem in metal and beneath it the black-white-red cockade.

Reconstruction of the sleeve badge. The colors of the badge have not been determined. The death's head emblem was unauthorized, however it was worn by the von Jungschultz Cossack Regiment, which had no badge of its own.

Reconstruction of the sleeve badge; the legend above the skull has yet to be identified.

Cossack non-commissioned officer. On his garrison cap are the soutache cord and the Reich cockade, but the national emblem is missing. There is also no national emblem on the man's tunic. He wears German NCO shoulder straps and the badge of an acting squad leader on the collar (as per Directive 8000/42 of August 1942). The silver braid has been sewn onto the collar with no background. The belt is a Russian-made item. Note the death's head badge on the left sleeve, the upper edge of which is rounded.

Various forms of the badge are seen here. The Cossack in the center wears the arm shield with death's head in a dark color. He is the only one wearing the national emblem on his tunic and German Army collar patches. The man sitting on the right wears a black sleeve badge with a white death's head, white trim and white title. The Cossack on the left is wearing the version of the badge with slightly rounded upper edge. The numerous versions of the death's head badge suggest that they were printed or, less likely, handmade.

The sleeve badge worn by the Cossack in the center (reconstruction). The colors of the background and the death's head are not known.

The sleeve badge worn by the Cossack sitting on the right (reconstruction).

Cossack Grenadier Regiment 360

The metal sleeve badge of the Cossack regiment was made of nickel-plated iron sheet with a superimposed "F" of brass. The emblem varied in size, although the one depicted here was 62.5 mm long. It was sewed onto the sleeve of the tunic and overcoat. The available photographs depicting this badge suggest that it was worn only be members of the regiment and attached German personnel. The three color photographs from the magazine *Signal*, Issue 21 of November 1943, depict the commander and two members of Cossack Grenadier Regiment 360.

Major der Reserve Ewert von Renteln as commander of the Cossack Grenadier Regiment 360. This photograph was taken in late March 1944 in Charente-maritme (French Departement on the Atlantic Coast).

Arm shield of the collar patches Grenadier Regiment 360.

On Page 86 *Oberst* d.R. von Renteln wears the POA badge of the Russian Liberation Army. The badge was worn on the upper left sleeve, both in the 1st Cossack Division and the XV Cossack Cavalry Corps.

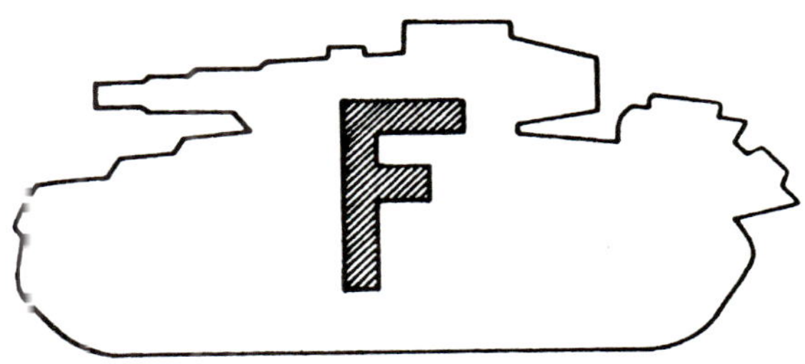

Metal badge, depicting a tank, marked with a letter "F".

Rittmeister, later *Oberst*, von Renteln, commander of the Cossack Grenadier Regiment 360. On his upper left sleeve he wears the badge of his regiment, beneath it a metal badge showing the silhouette of a Panzer III tank. The caption accompanying this picture reads: "When a *Hauptmann* and company commander, *Major* von Renteln, commander of a Cossack regiment, personally selected the personnel for his cadre company from numerous volunteers. On his left sleeve this old Baltic freedom fighter, called "Little Father" by his Cossacks, wears a silver tank with golden "F", the badge of honor of a panzer division at Rzhev."

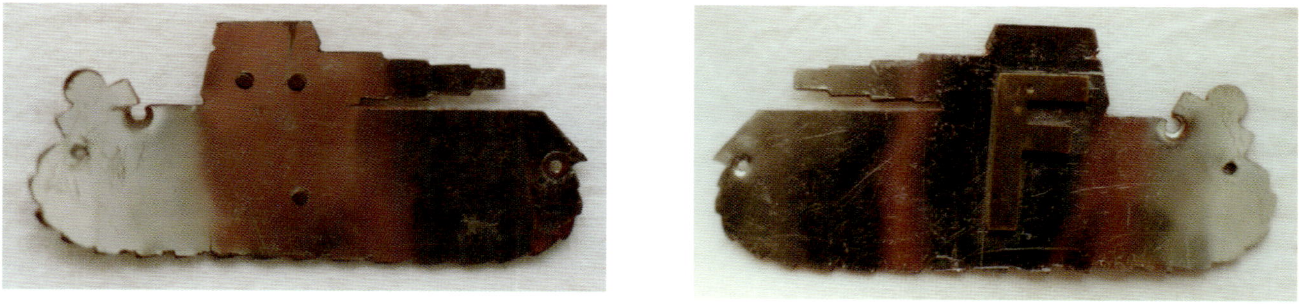

The metal tank badge. It has not been determined if it is an original.

A Cossack of the Cossack Grenadier Regiment 360. On the collar of his tunic are red collar patches with crossed lances.

An officer of the same regiment. His shoulder straps (Czarist type) show that he is a Headquarters *Rittmeister* (Podessaul).

Cossack Battalion 622

Cossack Battalion 623

Cossack Battalion 624

Cossack Battalion 625

The shoulder straps worn by this non-commissioned officer identify him as a "Company Commander" (as per the army directive of December 1942). On his upper left sleeve he wears a shield with two white stripes. The photograph was taken in early 1944 in the Atlantic defenses south of Bordeaux.

Fernspruch v. Rgt. am 24.10.44.

Ab 25.10.44. wird eine ständige Leibgarde für Herrn Rgt.-Kdeur.
befohlen zum ständigen Begleitschutz und zur Wachgestellung (Kdeur.)
Die Stärke : 1 Kos. Offz.
1 Kos. Uffz.
18 Kos.
Dazu werden kommandiert von Busenfreund 2 Kos.Meldung bis 25.10.44
bis 16,00 Uhr bei Herrn Rittm. Schabanow. Die Kommandierten sind im
tadellosen Anzug abzustellen.
Auf dem linken Oberarm haben die Angehörigen der Leibgarde einen grünen Winkel zu tragen.Senkrechte Höhe des Winkels 11 cm.(obere Breite
von Außenkante zu Außenkante gemessen,9 cm.Breite des Winkels 12 mm.

A teletype message sent by the regiment on 24 October 1944 concerning the formation of an independent bodyguard for *Oberst* Wagner. It specifies that the members of the bodyguard are to wear a green chevron on the upper left sleeve.

Cossack Battalion 624

Page 88 Bottom:
Sleeve badges of various Cossack battalions, reconstructed from photographs. These sleeve badges were worn on the upper arm and not in the 1st Cossack Division or XV Cossack Cavalry Corps.

Unknown Armshields

Sleeve chevron for members of the bodyguard of the commander of the Don Cossack Cavalry Regiment 1 (*Oberst* Wagner), formed at the end of October 1944. The chevron was an identity marking worn on the left upper sleeve of the tunic or coat.

Arm shield of an unidentified Cossack unit.

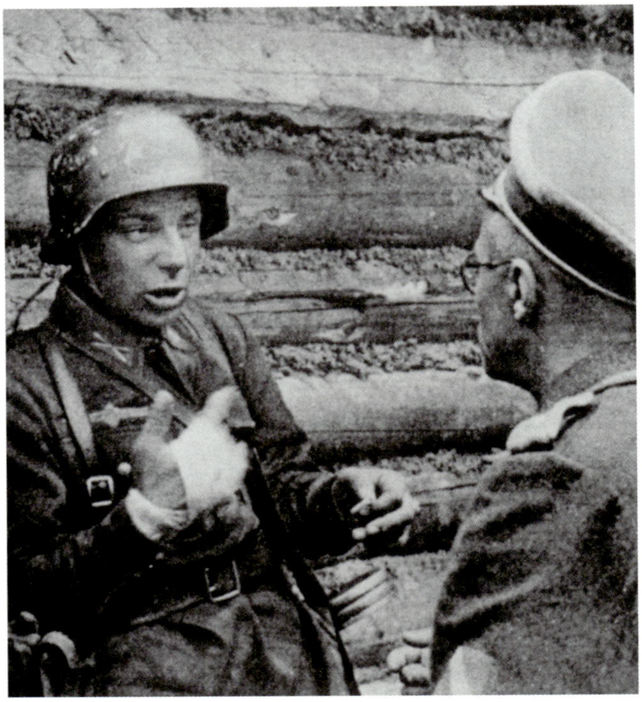

On the right an officer wearing the unidentified badge on the upper left sleeve. On the right breast of his tunic, the Cossack with the steel helmet is wearing the national emblem specified by Directive No. 8000/42 of August 1942 and the General Army Dispatches of 21 December 1942. Neither badge was worn in the 1st Cossack Division or the XV Cossack Cavalry Corps.

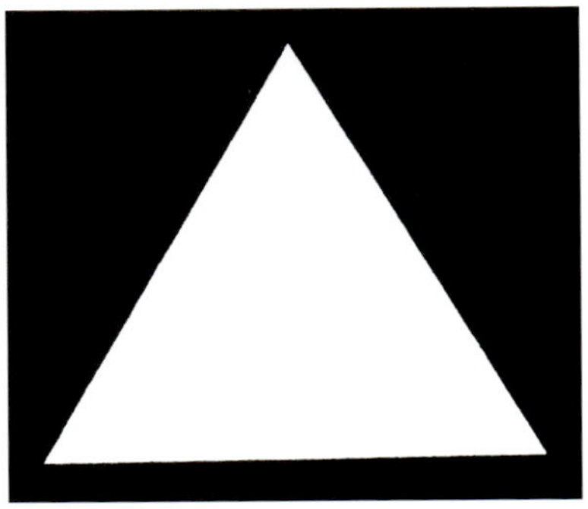

Left: Sleeve badge of an unidentified Cossack unit in the shape of an equilateral triangle. The badge was worn on the upper left sleeve.

The soldier on the right is wearing the white triangle on the left sleeve of his coat. Time and location where this photograph was taken are not known.

Emblems of the Young Cossacks and Cossack Officer Cadets

The young Cossacks were brought together in a Young Cossack Training Battalion or "Troop". Those who performed especially well were attached to a field unit of a Cossack army for a short time.

Their uniform was that of the former Army Non-Commissioned Officer Preschools. The German Army established non-commissioned officer preschools in 1940, however these were gradually disbanded in the period from 1941 to 1944. As the uniforms worn by the students of these schools (*Jungschützen*) had become surplus, they were passed on to the Young Cossacks.

The NCO preschool uniform included plain buttons and special collar patches outlined in white or pale green. The shoulder straps were also trimmed in white or pale green with the Gothic letters "UV" (for *Unteroffiziervorschule*) and beneath them the Roman numeral of the *Wehrkreis* in which the school was located.

The main administration of the Cossack Army was located in Northern Italy under the command of General P.N. Krasnov. The following Cossack schools were established there:

Cossack Officer Candidate School with four battalions
Cossack Cadet Corps with two troops
Cossack Military School with 180 students
Cossack Officer School with 180 students
Military College with 180 students
Girls College with 180 students
8 kindergartens and one other special school which bore the name "Ataman."

Mielau, 2 September 1943. The Young Cossacks on parade on the occasion of a visit by General P.N. Krasnov. The young men are wearing the non-commissioned officer preschool uniform with the "Unteroffiziervorschule" sleeve band.

Sleeve band of the NCO Preschoolers, worn by the Young Cossacks in the beginning. It is not known until when this sleeve band was worn on their uniforms.

"Young Cossacks School" sleeve band (reconstruction). The lettering is aluminum thread sewn onto a dark green band. Date of introduction is not known.

Mielau, September 1943. General Krasnov inspects the Young Cossacks.

Mokhov (near Mielau), summer 1943: young Cossacks and their instructors marching. At this point they are wearing the uniform of the non-commissioned officer preschool.

General von Pannwitz with the young Cossack Boris Nabokov, whom he adopted. On the right sleeve of the young man's coat is the sleeve band of the non-commissioned officer preschool. He wears the single-breasted coat of a student. A gold or silver chevron is visible on the lower left sleeve of his coat. In the non-commissioned officer preschool his identified the oldest boy in the room or class. General Pannwitz had earlier commanded the 2nd Battalion of the 11th Cavalry Regiment in Stockerau, Vienna and on his head he wears the fur cap of the Austrian Dragoons of the Federal Army (which ceased to exist in 1938). Many of the former officers of the 11th Cavalry Regiment who served in the 1st Cossack Division wore this fur cap.

Mielau, 2 Sept. 1943: The man on the right of the photo saluting is the troop leader of the Young Cossacks. He wears the Cossack collar patches on his tunic. Unfortunately it is impossible to tell if they are with or without crossed lances.

Young Cossack badge. The inscription is abbreviated, but identical to that on the armband, and reads: "Young Cossacks School". The badge depicted here is a copy. Unfortunately the author was unable to obtain an original. The badge was awarded for a certain number of front-line situations and after completion of the school. It was only worn on the dress uniform (when available).

General Michail Salamachin, commander of the Cossack cadet School in Italy.

A group of Cossack officer cadets. This photograph was most likely taken in northern Italy at the beginning of 1945. The Domanov Corps was also stationed there. Note the broad shoulder straps of the Cossack cadets. They are similar to the shoulder straps worn by non-commissioned officers of the *Wehrmacht* but were wider with rectangular instead of rounded corners. The cadets wear a variety of headgear: German garrison caps, caps similar to those worn in the days of the Czars, and kubankas. The Cossack officer cadet in the center of the photograph is wearing a *Waffen-SS* tunic, the result of a delivery of material from the *Waffen-SS*.

The Domanov Cossack Corps

The photographs presented here were taken in 1944-45 in Tolmezzo in northern Italy, where the corps headquarters was stationed. The corps was attached to the police.

The Cossack on the left is wearing a *Wehrmacht* coat, the one on the right a tunic without badges.

The Cossack on the left is wearing a tunic of the German Police. The tunic worn by the man on the right had probably been dyed.

Two military policemen of the Domanov Corps. Both men are wearing *Waffen-SS* tunics without collar patches but with SS sleeve badges and Cossack shoulder straps. On their kubankas is the Police National Emblem.

Cossacks distributing bread following an anti-partisan action Standing next to the army NCO is an SS-Scharführer.

The Culture and Entertainment Platoon of the 1st Cossack Division

In autumn 1943 in Mielau a culture and entertainment platoon was established for the 1st Cossack Division. While the Culture and Entertainment Platoon (Propaganda Platoon) was part of the division or corps headquarters, tactically it was attached to Division Reconnaissance Battalion 55. Active within this propaganda platoon was the war artist Olaf Jordan. Not only did the culture and entertainment platoon of the 1st Cossack Division and later the XV Cossack Cavalry Corps put out a front-line newspaper (Cossacks Illustrated), it also printed leaflets, placards and information sheets for the Cossacks.

Croatia, 1944. AN NCO of the Propaganda Platoon in front of a wall board bearing posters and leaflets.

Poster (text is in Serbian): "The Cossacks watch over 361 kilometers of railroad track, thus guaranteeing a significant level of trade and industry in the independent state of Croatia, as well as the transport of food and various other necessities."

Poster (text in Serbian)
Would you like to follow this path too?
That was we!
Free farmers on their native soil.
Happy people in a rich land.
Bulwark of the Russian people on the edge of the hostile steppe.

Bolshevism had destroyed:
our self-government,
our personal freedom,
our possessions, our families,
our traditions, our future.

Had you endured for twenty years this bloody path of tears and slavery as we did, you too would be fanatical fighters against Bolshevism and Jewry!

Head title of the "Cossack Illustrated." The following ten photographs are taken from issue No. 1/1944.

Croatia. A Cossack wearing the Decoration for Bravery for Members of the Eastern Peoples and the Croatian Zvonimir Medal manning a machine-gun position.

Croatia. Cossacks in action against partisans.

Cossacks marching.

Cossacks in formation.

Croatia. Cossacks riding on tanks.

Croatia. Cossacks resting.

"The General is here too" (says the caption). The dancing Cossack in the center is General Shkuro. In the background, clapping in time, officers and men of the 1st Cossack Division. Second from the left is *Generalleutnant* von Pannwitz.

Following the railroad tracks past a bunker.

"361 kilometers of railroad tracks belonging to the Croatian state are under your protection."

"Goodbye Father!"

The War Artist Olaf Jordan

Herr Stanislav Ausky succeeded in tracking down the works of the painter Olaf Jordan in a US Army archive in 1981. Among a large collection of seized art bearing the title "Nazi art", he found the works of the painter Jordan, a total of 28 paintings.

Olaf Jordan was born in the village of Birkigt in the Sudetenland on 10 March 1902. He studied at the Dresden Academy of Art from 1920 to 1925. His portraits went on display in Belgrade, Prague and Dresden. In mid-October 1942 he joined the Propaganda Section of fine artists as a painter. That year he gained notice as a war painter with four portraits of Yugoslavian prisoners of war. In 1943 he was attached to the Mielau troop training grounds in East Prussia. Located there was the camp and training center of the Cossacks. His first portraits of Cossacks were done at that time. In 1944 he crossed Yugoslavia with the 1st Cossack Cavalry Division. His best-known Cossack portraits were done in this period. During that time he painted just two Germans, *Leutnant* Nicolaus Regehr, his superior in the propaganda platoon, and *General* von Pannwitz. Aside from his portraits he completed a single sketch, Horses under Trees, in Kutina.

After the war Olaf Jordan and his wife and children were not spared the fate of expulsion. His wife (a native of Sweden) and children emigrated to Sweden. Olaf Jordan was released from captivity in July 1945 and followed his family. Everything he had, including his paintings, was lost. It was said that Cossack portraits were offered for sale after the war by a person who had been very close to the painter during the war. What is certain is that Jordan's works from the period from the end of 1944 to the beginning of 1945 are missing. It is due to the efforts of Herr Stanislav Ausky that the unique works of this artist have not been forgotten. It is for this reason that the author has included the following twenty portraits, which are of significance not just to military historians.

Olaf Jordan

Generalleutnant Helmuth von Pannwitz, commander of the 1st Cossack Division of the German Armed Forces, from 1 February 1945 commanding general of the XV Cossack Cavalry Corps of the *Waffen-SS*. On 28 May 1945 the Cossacks and their general were handed over to the Russians by British forces. In the Soviet Union von Pannwitz was sentenced to death and was executed in Moscow on 16 January 1947. On 23 April 1996 he was rehabilitated by the Chief State Prosecutor's Office of the Russian Federation.

Cossacks of the Guard Troop

Cossacks of the Guard Troop

Oberst Ivan Nikitich Kononov, commander of the Don Cossack Cavalry Regiment 5.

Cossack Luchkin of the Don Cossack Cavalry Regiment 5. Luchkin was Colonel Kononov's lifeguard Cossack.

Cossacks of the Don Cossack Cavalry Regiment 1 or 5.

Leutnant Ivan Nikitovic Sereda of the Kuban Cossack Cavalry Regiment 4 (visible above the armband is the strip of gold braid, the qualification badge of the Cossacks).

Leutnant Nikolaus Regehr, leader of the Culture and Entertainment Platoon.

Ataman Nikichwor Simonyenko of the Kuban Army.

The Ataman of the Terek Army, *Oberst* Nikolai Lazarovich Kulakov.

Cossacks of the Siberian Cossack Cavalry Regiment 2.

Cossacks

Cossacks

The Trumpet Corps of the 1st Cossack Division

The trumpet corps of the 1st Cossack Division and the later XV Cossack Cavalry Corps came from *Kavallerie-Regiment 11* (Stockau/Vienna). Many officers and men of *Kav.-Rgt. 11* served as cadre personnel in the 1st Cossack Division. For this reason the trumpet corps also used the drum trimmings and fanfare colors of that regiment. The 1st Cossack Division's parade march was the Prince Eugen March.

The trumpet corps' kettle drummer.

Division pope of the 1st Cossack Division.

The Clergy of the 1st Cossack Division

In the book *The History of the XV Cossack Cavalry Corps* by *Oberst* von Kalben, former commander of Terek Cossack Cavalry Regiment 6, the author relates that it was announced that the regimental popes (Russian Orthodox Church) of the 1st Cossack Division were to be eliminated. From his area of operations in Yugoslavia, *Generalmajor* von Pannwitz reported to his headquarters: "There are approximately 40,000 believing Protestants, Roman Catholics and Greek Orthodox, Muslims, Shintoists and Buddhists in my corps. They are accustomed to saying a prayer before going into battle. If my request is not granted, I fear difficulties of a religious nature." The response was, "Clergy of all creeds are authorized."

Generalmajor von Pannwitz with the division pope of the 1st Cossack Division.

The division pope blesses *General* Krasnov. Mielau, 943.

Cossack pay books.

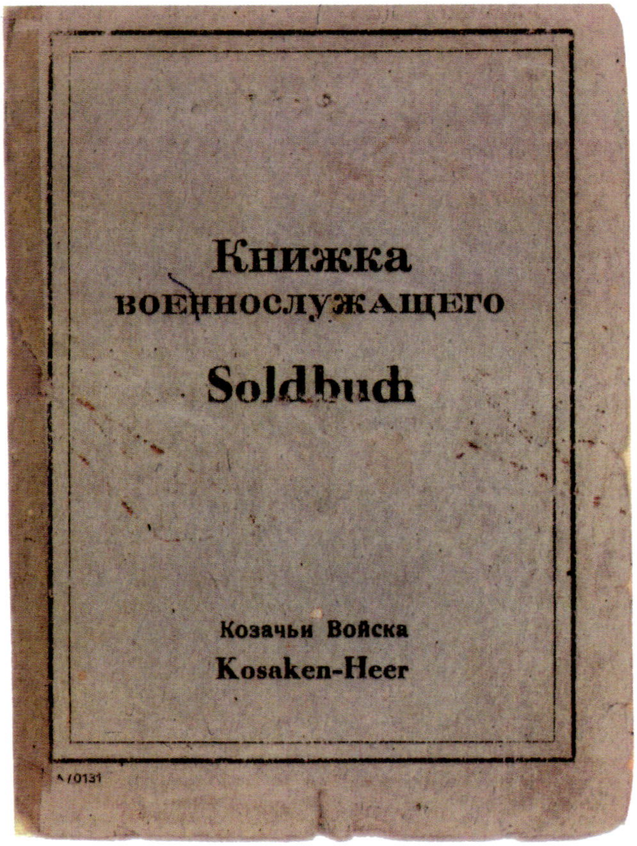
Книжка
военнослужащего
Soldbuch
Козачьи Войска
Kosaken-Heer

Фотография. Lichtbild.
Собств. подпись. Eigenhändige Unterschrift.
Применение полевого почтового номера в связи с означением военной части запрещается.
Gebrauch von F. P. N. neben offener Truppenbezeichnung ist verboten.

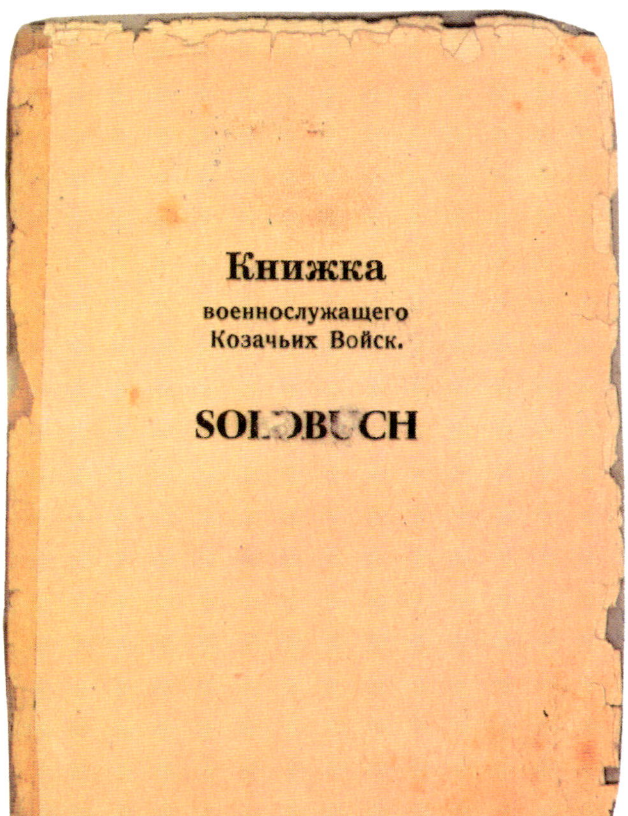
Книжка
военнослужащего
Козачьих Войск.
SOLDBUCH

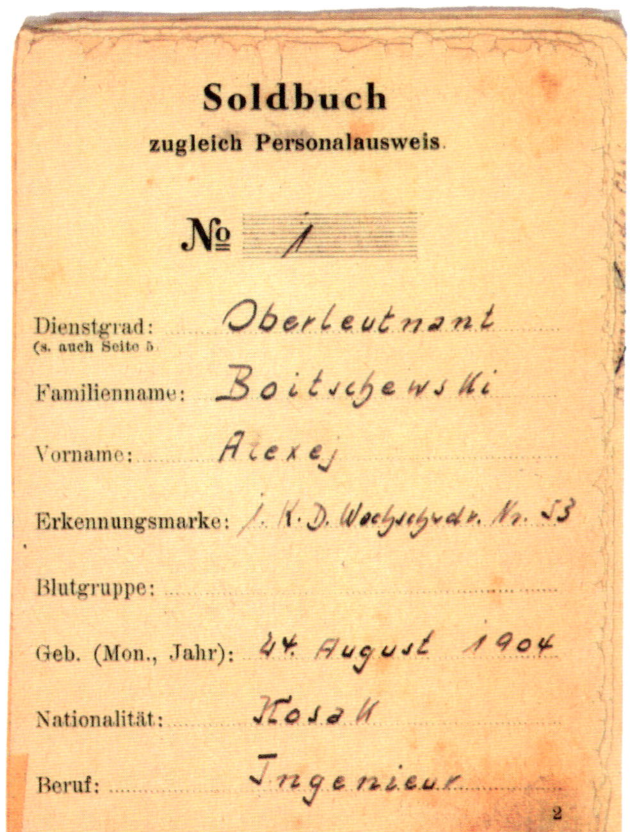
Soldbuch
zugleich Personalausweis
№ 1
Dienstgrad: Oberleutnant
(s. auch Seite 5)
Familienname: Boitschewski
Vorname: Alexej
Erkennungsmarke: 1. K. D. Wachschwdr. Nr. 53
Blutgruppe:
Geb. (Mon., Jahr): 24 August 1904
Nationalität: Kosak
Beruf: Ingenieur
2

The Cossack pay book was printed in the Russian and German languages. The example depicted here is the pay book of the former commander of the Guard Troop of the 1st Cossack Division. Shown are the cover, inside of cover with photograph, and the first, second and third pages. In addition to the usual entries such as personal information, decorations and promotions, there is a note stating that Oblt. Boychevsky is a member of the 1st Cossack Division and that he is entitled to wear the traditional Russian cherkesska and German shoulder straps.

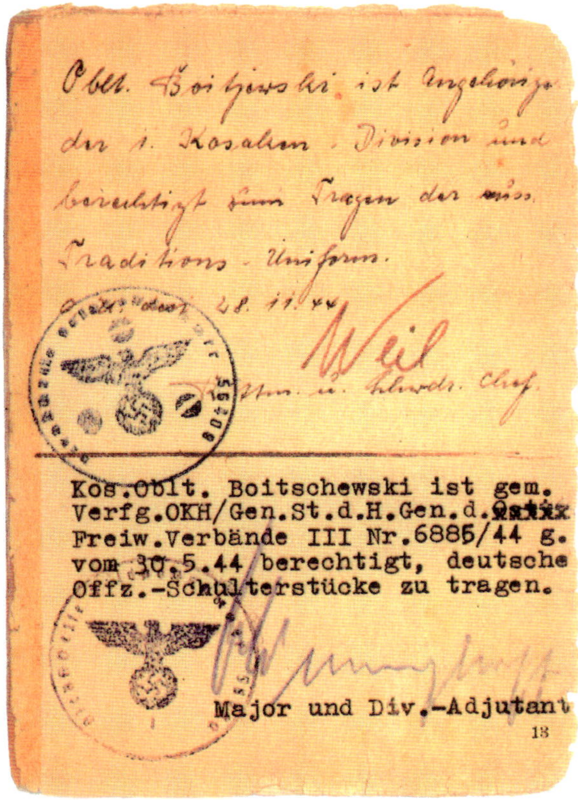
Oblt. Boitjewski ist Angehöriger der 1. Kosaken-Division und berechtigt zum Tragen der russ. Traditions-Uniform.

28. 11. 44

Weil

Kos.Oblt. Boitschewski ist gem. Verfg.OKH/Gen.St.d.H.Gen.d.Freiw.Verbände III Nr.6885/44 g. vom 30.5.44 berechtigt, deutsche Offz.-Schulterstücke zu tragen.

Major und Div.-Adjutant

13

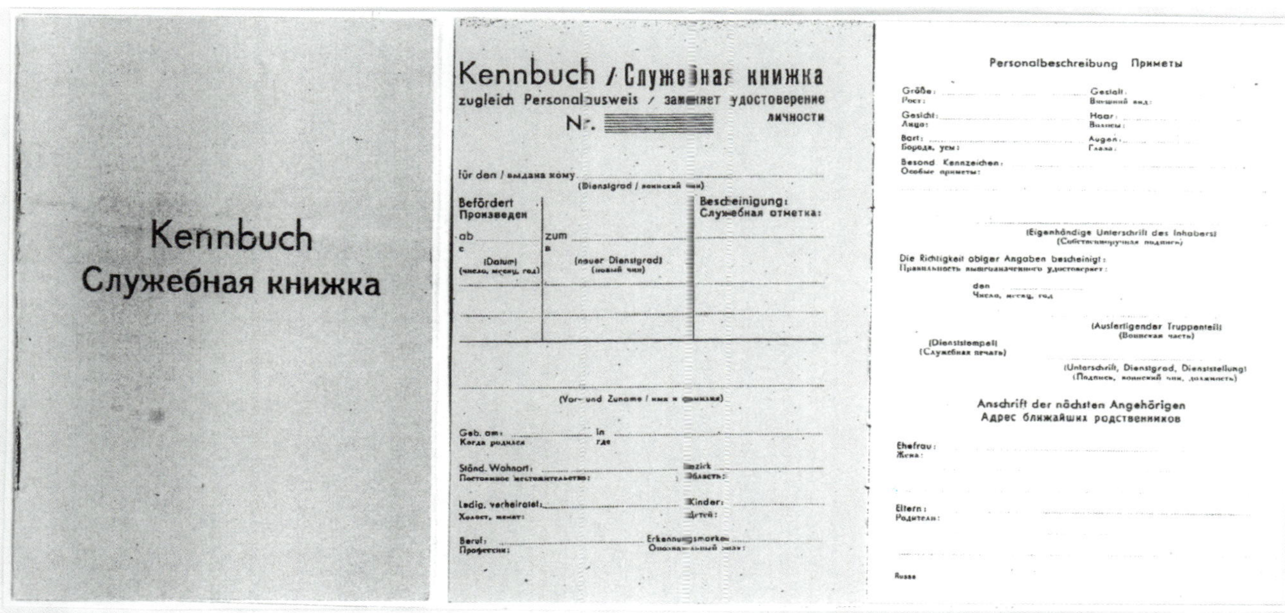
Kennbuch
Служебная книжка

Kennbuch / Служебная книжка
zugleich Personalausweis / заменяет удостоверение личности
Nr.

für den / выдана кому
(Dienstgrad / воинский чин)
Befördert / Произведен
ab / с
zum / в
(Datum) (число, месяц, год)
(neuer Dienstgrad) (новый чин)
Bescheinigung: / Служебная отметка:
(Vor- und Zuname / имя и фамилия)
Geb. am: / Когда родился
in / где
Ständ. Wohnort: / Постоянное местожительство:
Bezirk / Область:
Ledig, verheiratet: / Холост, женат:
Kinder: / Детей:
Beruf: / Профессия:
Erkennungsmarke:

Personalbeschreibung / Приметы
Größe: / Рост:
Gestalt: / Внешний вид:
Gesicht: / Лицо:
Haar: / Волосы:
Bart: / Борода, усы:
Augen: / Глаза:
Besond. Kennzeichen: / Особые приметы:
(Eigenhändige Unterschrift des Inhabers) (Собственноручная подпись)
Die Richtigkeit obiger Angaben bescheinigt:
den / Число, месяц, год
(Ausfertigender Truppenteil) (Воинская часть)
(Dienststempel) (Служебная печать)
(Unterschrift, Dienstgrad, Dienststellung)
Anschrift der nächsten Angehörigen
Адрес ближайших родственников
Ehefrau: / Жена:
Eltern: / Родители:
Russe

Like the pay book, the identity pass was also printed in Russian and German. The one illustrated here has no entries. Shown here is the front cover and the first two pages.

Identity Disks

As members of the German armed forces, the Cossacks carried the standard pay book plus the identity disk.

The identity disks illustrated here were made of aluminum or zinc. On the reverse side (not illustrated) there were other numbers whose purpose is not known.

The abbreviations on this identity disc mean: 1st Cossack Division, 8th Troop Kuban Cossack Cavalry Regiment 4, personnel roster number 91. This disc is made of zinc.

Personnel roster number 11344, Cossack Cadre Regiment/ Headquarters Section. The Cossack Cadre Regiment was the replacement training unit of the 1st Cossack Division. Identity disc of zinc.

Identity disc of Cossack Police Troop 7, personnel roster number 412. No data is stamped on the reverse side.

The *Bulava*

The *bulava* is a war club or hand weapon from the Middle Ages in the form of a cudgel with iron spines. It resembled the "Morning Star." Later the *bulava* was used as a scepter and served as a social emblem of the Atamans. It was produced in various forms. There were examples made of iron, precious metals and wood. The most common type was a shaft with a richly decorated silver knob. In its simpler forms, the *bulava* was also a type of commander's baton of the Stanitsa District and the Chutor Atamans (*stanitsa* = a Cossack fortified settlement, later equivalent to a district village in Russia; the Stanitsa District was equivalent to a city; *chutor* = farm, farmhouse with associated buildings).

From left to right: Iron bulava, length 52 cm; decorated bulava of iron, bronzed head, length 57.4 cm; iron bulava with gold decoration. Length 70.4 cm. This bulava dates from 1753. A Latin dedication is engraved on the grip. A wooden bulava, painted and gilded. Length 56 cm.

Cossack Whips

As Cossacks traditionally did not wear spurs, they urged their horses on with the whip, or *nagaika*. Cossack officers had worn spurs from the time of the Czars, however they also carried the *nagaika*, most of which were handmade and of high quality.

Wooden nagaika.

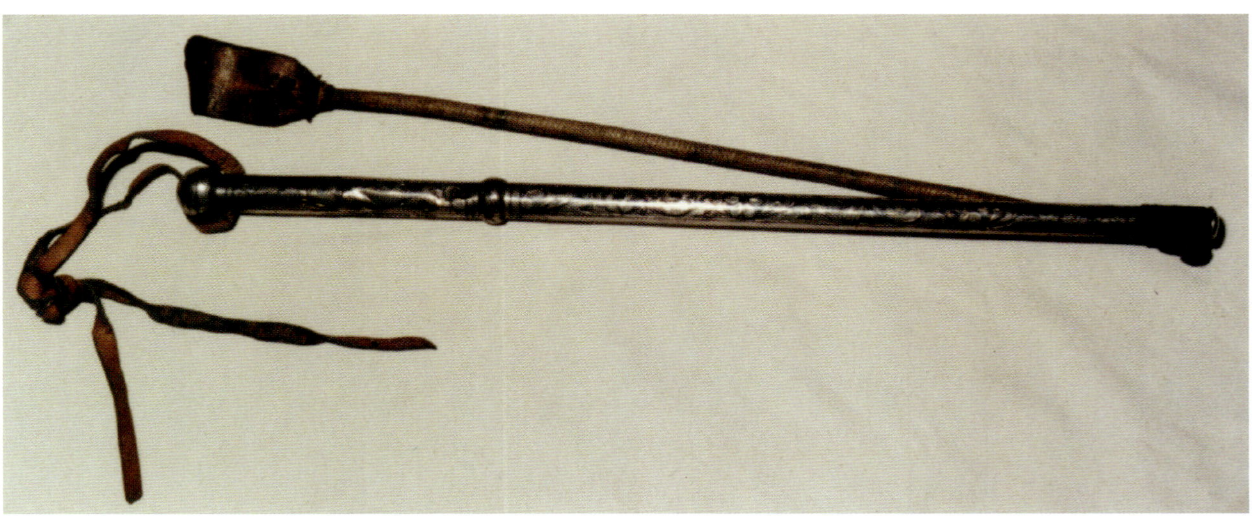

The nagaika depicted here is made of silver. Inside the long shaft is a stiletto.

Another nagaika with silver fittings. The fittings are of Niello silver. Carved or etched grooves were filled with black Niello metal and then smoothed and polished.

Oberst von Bosse and *Oberst* Kononov. In his right hand *Oberst* Kononov holds a silver nagaika.

Pljotka

The plyotka, a short pleated whip used by the Cossacks. Plyotka is Russian for "The Pleated One."

Cossack Sabers

Both types of saber, Caucasian and Don, were worn by the Cossacks, on the *pojas*, or belt, with the *cherkesska*, and on the crossbelt with the *Wehrmacht* uniform. The *shashkas* illustrated are the Don type, which were worn only by the Don Cossacks. In the 1st Cossack Division and the XV Cossack Cavalry Corps these types of saber were also worn by the Cossacks of other regiments (Kuban, Terek and Siberian) and by members of the Guard Troop. The bayonet clip was introduced in the time of the Czars for horse-drawn units only (train units and horse-artillery). As the Cossacks fighting on the side of the Germans did not use the bayonet, the upper and lower scabbard bands were removed, leaving just the band with the carrying ring. At the top of the iron or brass pommel (the so-called cleft with the two ears) was a round hole, through which was pulled the leather or cord sword knot.

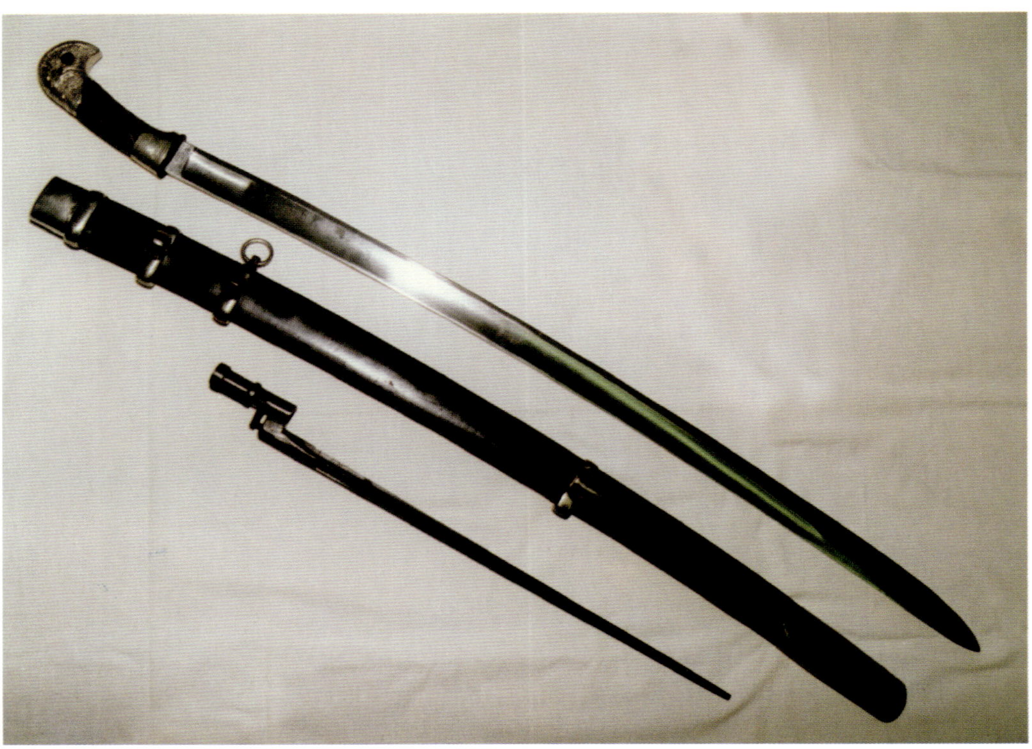

Cavalry shashka model 1927 (here fitted with sliding bands on the scabbard for a bayonet).

Cossack saber (Don type), Model 1900. Here the sliding bands have been removed. The saber is fitted with carrying sling and hand loop.

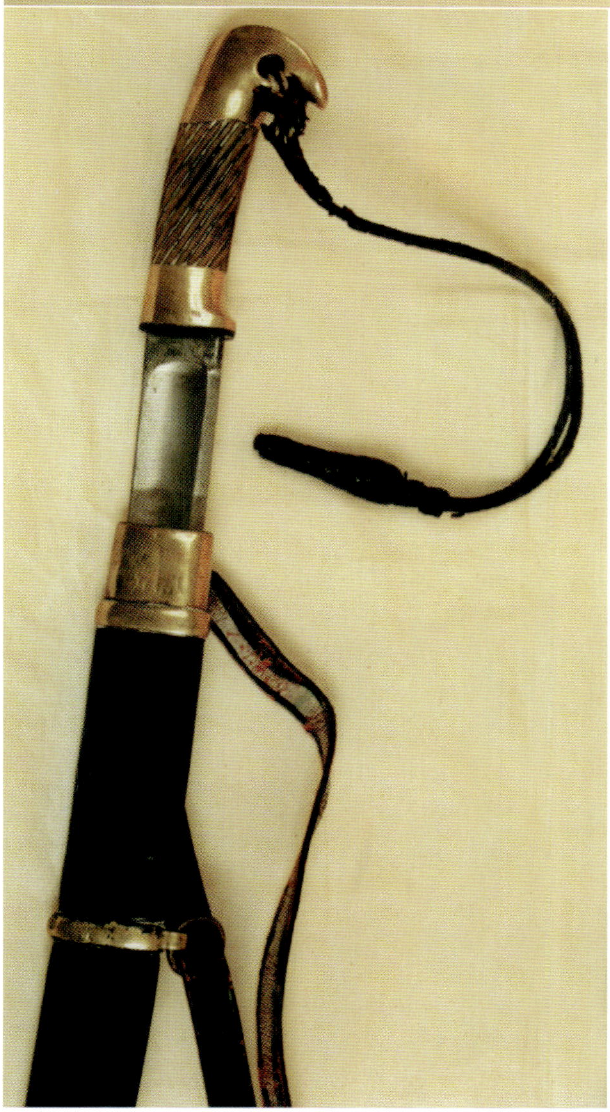

A German Wachtmeister attached to a Cossack unit. He is seen wearing the shashka in the prescribed manner. The saber is attached to the carrying sling, which is worn under the *Wehrmacht* belt.

The stock was made of wood and ribbed diagonally. Cossack sabers made after the October Revolution featured a large Soviet emblem in relief on the front side of the pommel, a five-pointed star with the hammer and sickle. Most members of Cossack units removed this emblem.

The carrying lugs and rings of Cossack sabers were on the side of the scabbard (old Slavic carriage), so that the saber hung on the hip with the scabbard facing up.

Caucasian-Type Cossack Sabers

The blade is slightly curved, with two concavings on each side of the blade. The bone grip is black, attached with three rivets, ending in a typical pommel. A saber of this type is depicted in Olaf Jordan's portrait of *Oberst* Kononov. The scabbard is leather covered with a silver fitting. The scabbard throat is extended to such a degree that the saber can be inserted almost to the pommel. In the Russian Army this weapon was used by the Cossacks from the Terek and Kuban and by the Czar's bodyguard.

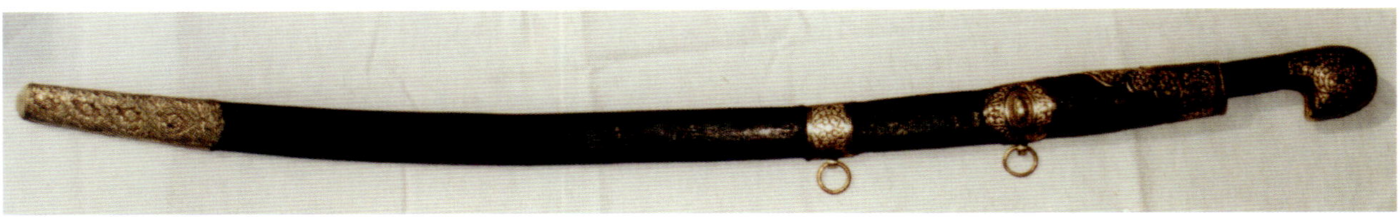

These photographs illustrate the different levels of workmanship and materials employed in producing the Cossack saber of the Caucasian type. The shashka at the top has a silver-trimmed scabbard, while the other two have black leather scabbards with some gold fittings.

Circassian *Kindshal*

The blade of this typical Caucasian stabbing weapon is straight, varying in length from approximately 30 cm, with a very pointed tip. The way the concavings are ground into the blade is very interesting. Usually they are staggered on opposite sides of the blade. Sometimes, however, they appear in larger numbers and are directly opposite each other. The grip has an outer covering of bone or horn or is made entirely of silver. The scabbard is made of wood and is covered with leather and trimmed with silver, or in more elaborate versions is sheathed entirely in silver. The metal throat always has a band with a carrying handle, while the scabbard is tipped with a ball. This weapon is an integral part of the Caucasian male's attire. Most *kindshals* have a straight blade, although in rare cases the blade is curved.

Above: This photograph (taken in Croatia in 1944) shows members of the Guard Troop of the 1st Cossack Division with sabers presented. The Wachtmeister on the left has attached the scabbard of his shashka to the German Army cross belt (with hooks and eyes).

Rittmeister Boychevsky wearing the Caucasian type saber on his pojas (belt). The pommel is the only part of the saber projecting from the scabbard.

Generals Shkuro and Naumenko, both wearing the kindshal (dagger) at the front on their belts.

A kindshal with silver fittings.

A kindshal with black leather scabbard. The handle is made of bone.

An ornate kindshal; handle and scabbard have been gilded.

A kindshal with silver fittings. The sheath is trimmed with red velvet.

Decorations Awarded to Cossacks

Bravery and Meritorious Service Decorations for Members of the Eastern Peoples

With the introduction of German rank badges, Cossacks also began receiving German decorations. A "Bravery and Meritorious Service Decoration for Members of the Eastern Peoples" was created on 14 July 1942. The decoration consisted of an eight-pointed star with a round central shield, on which was a sun wheel surrounded by a laurel wreath. The first class of the decoration was pinned on the left breast of the service coat, while the second class decoration was worn on a ribbon above the left breast pocket. When awarded for bravery, the medal had crossed swords above the star. The first class medal was awarded in gold and silver, the second class in gold, silver and bronze. The ribbon for the gold level was pale green with narrow red stripes, for the silver level medium green with narrow white stripes, and for the bronze level plain dark green.

Each decoration of the second grade could be awarded up to three times. A similar regulation had existed in Czarist Russia. German personnel attached to Cossack units were also eligible to receive the decoration. The Iron Cross, First Class was required in order to receive the first class decoration, the Iron Cross, Second Class for the second class. In general, only the silver levels of the first and second class decorations were awarded to German personnel. In a few exceptional cases German personnel received the first class in gold. Before the Cossacks were eligible to receive the Iron Cross, they were awarded the War Merit Cross with Swords as a medal of bravery.

Meritorious Service Decoration Second Class in Bronze.

Meritorious Service Decoration Second Class in Silver.

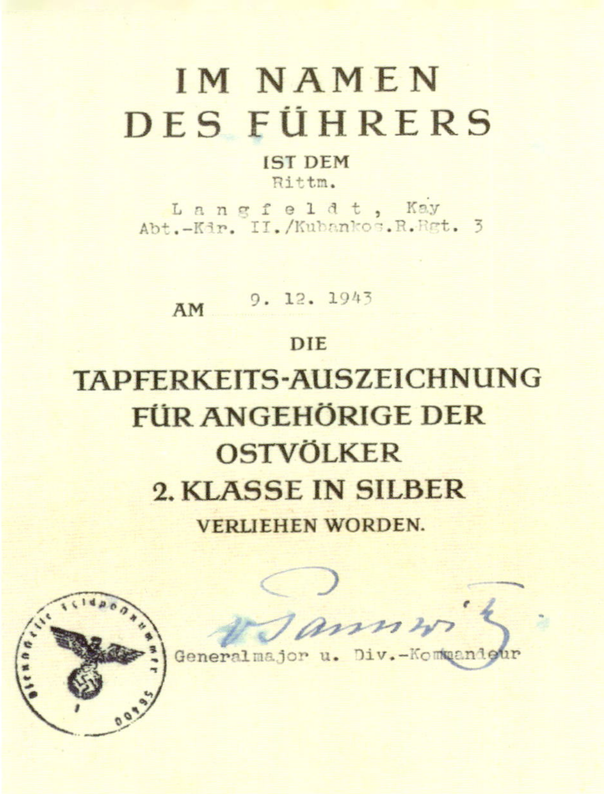

IM NAMEN
DES FÜHRERS
IST DEM
Rittm.
L a n g f e l d t , Kay
Abt.-Kdr. II./Kubankos.R.Rgt. 3
AM 9. 12. 1943
DIE
TAPFERKEITS-AUSZEICHNUNG
FÜR ANGEHÖRIGE DER
OSTVÖLKER
2. KLASSE IN SILBER
VERLIEHEN WORDEN.

v Pannwitz
Generalmajor u. Div.-Kommandeur

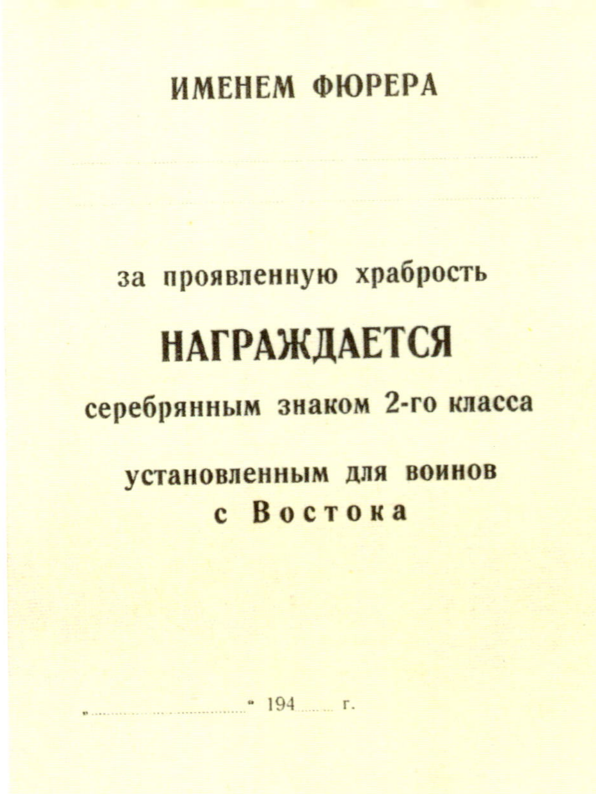

ИМЕНЕМ ФЮРЕРА

за проявленную храбрость
НАГРАЖДАЕТСЯ
серебрянным знаком 2-го класса
установленным для воинов
с Востока

„..........“ 194.... г.

Front and rear of an award certificate for the Bravery Decoration for Members of the Eastern Peoples, Second Class, in Silver to the commander of the 2nd Battalion, Kuban Cossack Cavalry Regiment 3, Kay Langfeldt. The certificate is signed by *Generalmajor* von Pannwitz, commander of the 1st Cossack Division.

Bravery Decoration Second Class in Bronze

Meritorious Service Decoration Second Class in Gold

Bravery Decoration Second Class in Silver

Croatia, late 1943. Cossacks of the 1st Battalion of the Kuban Cossack Cavalry Regiment 4 receive decorations.

The Cossacks after receiving their Decorations Second Class for Members of the Eastern Peoples. Note the variety of headgear.

Bravery Decoration First Class in Silver

Cossack officer of the Kuban Cossack Cavalry Regiment 3. On his kubanka is the small metal death's head of the armored forces (Panzertruppe). Visible on the row of cartridge holders on his cherkesska are the Bravery Decoration First Class (Silver or Gold?) and the wound badge.

General von Pannwitz decorates members of the Guard Troop.

General von Pannwitz pins the Iron Cross Second Class onto the uniform of a Cossack soldier.

Regimental Cross of the Siberian Cossack Cavalry Regiment 2

This cross was established in March 1944, the first anniversary of the creation of the Siberian Cossack Cavalry Regiment 2 by *Oberst-leutnant* Baron von Nolcken, the regiment's commander. It was presented as a commemorative cross. There was no award document, and an entry was made in the recipient's pay book stating that he was entitled to wear the decoration. The letters on the shield which adorns the cross stand for: left: Polk; center: Sibirski; right Voyna Voysky (Siberian War Regiment).

Regimental Cross of the Don Cossack Cavalry Regiment 5

Oberstleutnant Kononov created this cross in the summer of 1944 as a tradition or souvenir badge for his Don Cossack Cavalry Regiment 5. The number 5 on the upper bar of the cross represents the regiment, the Cyrillic script on the left and right bars is the name of *Oberstleutnant* Kononov, and the numbers on the lower bar form the date 28.X.1941 (formation of the 102nd Cossack Regiment). There was no award certificate for this regimental cross, and no entry was made in the recipient's pay book.

In August 1941 the then Major Kononov defected to the Germans with his 436th Infantry Regiment. From this regiment was initially formed the 102nd Cossack Regiment. Since Russian units were only approved in battalion strength, on 27 January 1942 the Cossack unit was renamed Cossack Battalion 600. This change in designation did not result in any reduction in personnel strength. Indeed the opposite was true. An additional 1,000 men were added to the battalion's strength, which reached a total of almost 2,000. On 12 July 1943 the unit was again renamed, becoming Cossack Cavalry Regiment 5. At the end of 1944 Kononov was promoted to the rank of *Oberst*. In the spring of 1945 he went to the ROA and was promoted to *Generalmajor*.

Cossack officer of the Siberian Cossack Cavalry Regiment 2 with the regimental cross on the right breast pocket of his tunic. The ribbon of the Iron Cross, Second Class is incorrectly sewed. The cuffs are trimmed. The man is wearing czarist shoulder straps and the collar patches for officers on his collar.

Members of the 1st Cossack Division and other units in the rest home in Kirchberg in Tyrol. In the back row is a member of the Don Cossack Cavalry Regiment 5, wearing the commemorative cross on his right breast pocket.

Flags and Command Emblems of the Cossack Units

Kuban Cossacks on flag parade Photographed in Mielau.

Flags of the Kuban Cossacks (left), the Terek Cossacks (right) and the Don Cossacks (below). The flags of the Kuban and Terek Cossacks were similar in design to the sleeve badges worn by those groups.

Mielau, 1943, the guard house. On the right the German War Flag flies from the guard house. On the left is the flag of the Don Cossacks. It was created by the Don Cossacks in May 1918 during the Russian civil war. The sequence of colors is yellow-blue-red. These colors represent the main elements of the population of the Don Region: Kalmucks, Cossacks and farmers. The first sleeve badges worn by the Don Cossacks also used these colors.

Don Cossack Cavalry Regiment 1

The Don Cossack Cavalry Regiment 1 received its standard in Zagreb in May 1944. It was presented by the ethnic Germans in the Croatian capital and the Association of Former Russian Soldiers. The basic colors of the flag were those of the Don Army, blue and red. As the regiment was constantly in action and had little opportunity to show the flag, it remained packed in the regimental headquarters' ammunition and weapons wagon. The vehicle and the standard were later captured and burned by partisans.

The regimental headquarters of the Don Cossack Cavalry Regiment 1 used a square battle flag measuring approximately 60 by 60 centimeters. Against a plain yellow background on both sides, facing away from the mast, was a black leaping stag pierced by an arrow. The leaping stag was derived from an historical flag of the Don Cossacks. The statement made by the emblem was that not even a running stag could escape a Cossack arrow.

The headquarters of the 1st and 2nd Battalions of the Don Cossack Cavalry Regiment 1 each flew a yellow pennant with the emblem of the Don Army. The yellow pennant was shaped as an isosceles triangle. In the center, facing away from the mast, was the black stag pierced by an arrow. In the left upper corner next to the mast was a roughly equilateral triangle separated from the rest of the pennant by a diagonal black stripe. Inside was the battalion number, the Roman numeral I or II (according to Dr. Klietmann). The pennant was approximately 30 cm high and 40 cm long. These battle flags of the regimental and battalion headquarters were introduced toward the end of 1943 and were used until the end.

Don Cossacks on flag parade. This photograph appeared on the title page of Cossack Illustrated No. 2/1944.

Flag of the Don Cossacks, a drawing based on the photograph on the left.

Battle flag of the Don Cossack Cavalry Regiment 1.

Command pennant of the 2nd Battalion of the Don Cossack Cavalry Regiment 1. The battalion number appears on the top attachment loop.

Siberian Cossack Cavalry Regiment 2

In May 1944 the regiment received a standard from an association of former Imperial Russian soldiers in Belgrade or Srmska Mitrovitza. It was in the national colors yellow and blue. As well, the regimental headquarters flew the usual command flag in the colors black—gold yellow—black, with an Arabic number 2 in the yellow field.

On the right of the photograph the command pennant of the "von Bremen" Battalion headquarters in the Siberian Cossack Cavalry Regiment 2. The colors of the pennant are yellow-black-yellow, with white lettering.

Kuban Cossack Cavalry Regiment 3

The regimental headquarters flew the usual flag of the regimental commander: black—gold yellow—black, with an Arabic number 3 in the yellow field.

Kuban Cossack Cavalry Regiment 4

The regimental headquarters flew the usual flag of the regimental commander: black—gold yellow—black, with an Arabic number 4 in the yellow field.

Don Cossack Cavalry Regiment 5

The regimental headquarters flew the usual flag of the regimental commander: black—gold yellow—black, with an Arabic number 5 in the yellow field.

The headquarters of the 1st and 2nd Battalions of the Don Cossack Cavalry Regiment 5 also flew a command flag, produced as follows: a pennant with cutout, divided horizontally into two halves, the upper blue and the lower red. Roughly in the center of the blue field was a white Roman numeral I or II, depending on the battalion. While the flag was 100 cm long, its width was 60 cm and the depth of the cutout approximately 40 cm. The flag mast was approximately 40 mm in diameter.

The troops of the Don Cossack Cavalry Regiment 5 carried a pennant with a cutout in the center. The pennant was 65 cm long and 40 cm wide, the cutout 17 cm deep. All of these troop pennants were divided horizontally into two halves, with the bottom half in red and the top half in the troop color. In the center of the pennant was the troop number in white.

Command flag of Headquarters, 1st Battalion.

Command flag of Headquarters, 2nd Battalion.

Command pennant of the 1st Troop (green-red).

Command pennant of the 2nd Troop (yellow-red).

Command pennant of the 3rd Troop (white-red), length of pennant: 62 cm, height: 39 cm.

Command pennant of the 3rd Troop (white-red), command pennant of the 4th Troop (black-red).

5th Troop: green/red with a white Arabic 5
6th Troop: yellow/red with a white Arabic 6.
7th Troop: white/red with a white Arabic 7.
8th Troop: black/red with a white Arabic 8.
9th Troop: top color not known, bottom red (?) with a white Arabic 9.

Terek Cossack Cavalry Regiment 6

The regimental headquarters flew a special pennant in the shape and color of the usual headquarters flag of a cavalry regiment commander with one difference, namely the emblem on the yellow center field. The command flag of the regimental headquarters was attached to a cavalry lance with three bands. The flag was divided into three horizontal stripes of equal width in black, gold yellow and black. On the center field was the emblem of the 1st Cossack Division. Placed above the shield was a blue bar and beneath it a black one, these representing the colors of the Terek Cossacks.

Command flag of the regimental headquarters.

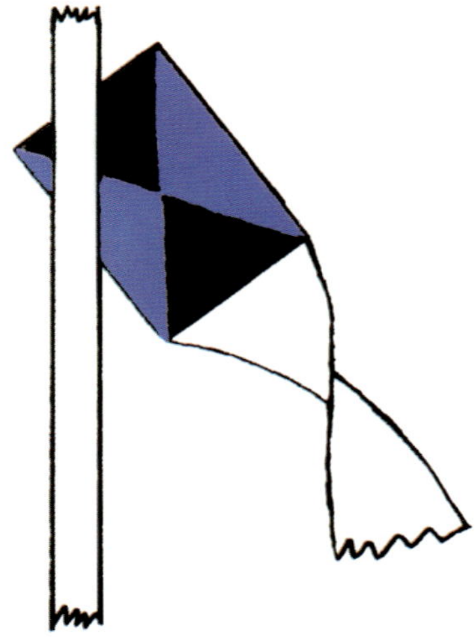

Reconstruction of the pennant band.

Croatia, July 1944. The regimental flag of the Terek Cossack Cavalry Regiment 6 flies from an old German lance. Beneath it is a pennant. The pennant is approximately 120 cm long and its upper end is in the colors of the Terek Cossack Cavalry Regiment 6: blue and black. This must have been the command flag of the regimental headquarters of the Terek Cossacks. Unfortunately, in the photograph on the left the escutcheon is not visible on the central yellow field. It may have been added later, or it may be on the other side of the flag and thus cannot be seen.

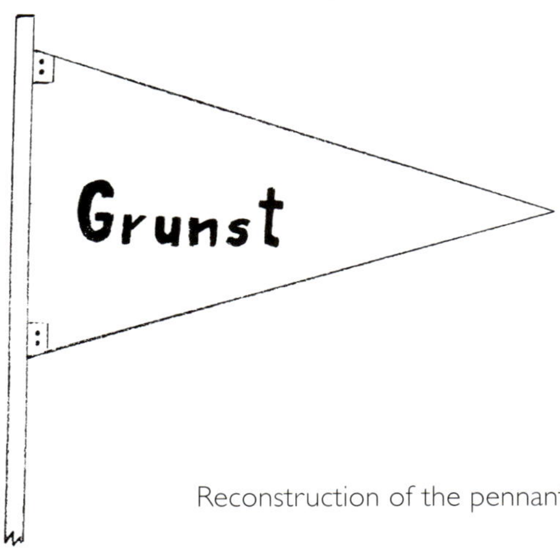

Reconstruction of the pennant.

Croatia, summer 1944. In the center of the photograph the command pennant of the 1st Battalion of the Terek Cossack Cavalry Regiment 6. Just visible on the pennant is the title "Grunst," the name of the battalion commander, *Major* Grunst. Unfortunately the color of the pennant is not known.

Croatia, January 1944. The vehicle of the commander of the Terek Cossack Cavalry Regiment 6. The two close-ups show two different command flags for the Terek Cossack Cavalry Regiment 6.
On the front left of the vehicle (above) and on the rear (below). The reason for the two different flags is not known. The colors of both flags are yellow-black-yellow.
Visible on the rear left side of the vehicle, a Tatra, is the tactical symbol of the 1st Cossack Division, and above it the colors of the Terek Cossack Cavalry Regiment 6: blue and black.

Croatia, 1944. General Shkuro visits the Terek Cossack Cavalry Regiment 6. On the steel tube lance is the general's standard, on which a wolf's head may be seen. When the Cossacks rose up against the Bolsheviks in the Russian Civil War, Shkuro commanded a regiment of three- to four-hundred horsemen who called themselves "Wolves." Like his horsemen, Shkuro wore a cap made of wolf fur instead of the usual fleece. His headquarters was in several rail cars. Painted on the outside of the cars was a wolf pack on the hunt.

Mielau, September 1943. The Cossacks on parade in honor of General Krasnov. In the center are members of the Cossack Training and Replacement Regiment. A swastika flag was carried on the right wing of the formation (just visible in the center of the photo). Visible in the foreground is an as yet unidentified pennant.

Reconstruction of the troop pennant.

Croatia. The photograph depicts assembled Cossacks of the Terek Cossack Cavalry Regiment 6 during the burial of fallen comrades. The pennant of the 1st Troop may be seen in the background.

Artillery Units of the 1st Cossack Division

The headquarters of the 1st (Mounted) Cossack Artillery Battalion 55 flew a command flag (probably from the summer of 1943 to July 1944) designed as follows: a pennant in the shape of an isosceles triangle. The fabric of the flag was blue with a narrow white outline. In the center was the legend "v. Eisenhardt-Rothe" in Latin script. Measurements may have been 30 x 60 cm. *Major* von Eisenhardt-Rothe commanded the battalion from 28 April 1943 until he was transferred to the officer reserve on 20 July 1944.

The headquarters of the 2nd (Mounted) Cossack Artillery Battalion 55 flew a pennant which resembled a headquarters flag of an artillery battalion of the German Army. The pennant measured 30 x 60 cm.

1st (Mounted) Cossack Artillery Battalion 55, headquarters command pennant.

2nd (Mounted) Cossack Artillery Battalion 55, headquarters command pennant. The significance of the Roman numeral I in the upper field of the pennant is unclear.

Flags of unidentified Cossack units

Standard of an unidentified Cossack unit. On the standard are a nagaika and a shashka, with a horseshoe above and a kubanka below.

The wording on this flag illustrates one of the most important motives which lead the Cossacks to fight against Communism and join the German armed forces. It reads: "In the name of Orthodox Christianity, the faithful sons of the Don join a determined struggle against the unbelievers."

The same flag from the other side. St. George is clearly visible in the center. At the top of the flag, left and right, are two eagles grasping the swastika in their talons.

North of the Caucasus, probably 1942. Cossacks of an unidentified unit with a swastika flag. Both Cossacks are wearing the cherkesska. The man on the left has a Soviet Tokarev 1940 automatic rifle slung across his back.

Reconstruction of the flag seen in the photograph below.

Photograph of an unidentified Cossack unit. The flag was probably black with a white death's head. The legend above the death's head probably reads "2nd Cossack Troop".

Mielau, September 1943. General Krasnov visits the 1st Cossack Division. Assembled for his inspection are the Young Cossacks. Note the swastika flag and the flag tip. There is an unidentified emblem in the top corner of the flag next to the mast. The flag tip may contain three oak leaves.

This photograph of an unidentified Cossack unit was probably taken in the Caucasus in 1943. Visible in the center of the photograph is a swastika flag. On the left of the photo is the unit's flag. The only words on the flag which may be read are the name Adolf Hitler on the left. Visible beneath the name are a reversed swastika and a half moon and star.

Identifying Markings on the Horses of the 1st Cossack Division

On 30 November 1943 the IVc Department (division veterinary officer) of the 1st Cossack Division prescribed identity markings for the unit's horses. The following markings were then applied on the edge of the left rear hoof:

Don Cossack Cavalry Regiment 1	O
Siberian Cossack Cavalry Regiment 2	S
Kuban Cossack Cavalry Regiment 3	M
Kuban Cossack Cavalry Regiment 4	–
Don Cossack Cavalry Regiment 5	K
Terek Cossack Cavalry Regiment 6	(*see text*)
1st Mounted Cossack Artillery Battalion	inverted V
2nd Mounted Cossack Artillery Battalion	V
Cossack Signals Battalion	I
Cossack Pioneer Battalion	II
Division Supply Troops	N

On the right rear hoof: the unit number preceded by the troop, battery or company number (e.g. 9./211 or I./370). Regimental and independent battalion headquarters had only the unit number.

Identity Markings on the Vehicles of the 1st Cossack Division

On 14 November 1943 an order was issued for the marking of motor vehicles and vehicles (meaning horse-drawn vehicles). Application of the new markings was to be confirmed to the Ib (2nd General Staff Officer-Supply Section) by 30 November. The marking of vehicles was carried out as follows:

Vehicles of all elements of the division bore the division emblem: two crossed Cossack sabers and the *bulava* in gold yellow on a pale blue shield.

Those of the regiments, battalions and independent battalions of the fighting units wore a 32- or 16-mm bar immediately above the shield in the following colors:

H.Q. 1st Cossack Cavalry Brigade	blue-yellow
H.Q. 2nd Cossack Cavalry Brigade	blue-red
Don Cossack Cavalry Regiment 1	blue-red
Siberian Cossack Cavalry Regiment 2	blue-yellow
Kuban Cossack Cavalry Regiment 3	black-red
Kuban Cossack Cavalry Regiment 4	red-black
Don Cossack Cavalry Regiment 5	red-blue
Terek Cossack Cavalry Regiment 6	blue-black

The first named color took up the upper 16 mm of the colored bar, the second the lower 16 mm. In each case where the lower color was blue, the bar was separated from the shield by a narrow white line. Units with a color wore the colored bar in a width of 16 mm: Pi.Btl. Black, Signals Btl. Lemon yellow, Artillery red.

In addition to the division emblem, the division supply units wore a tactical emblem in black as per H.Dv. 272.

Application of the emblem (by stencil):

	Motorcycles	Automobiles	Trucks	Horse-Drawn vehicles
Division emblem	Motorcycle-sidecars front and rear on sidecar	Front: right fender Rear: left fender or rear of vehicle	Front: right fender Rear: left side of tailgate or rear end.	Front: on the left sidewall, forward third Rear: left side of rear wall
Tactical emblem (supply units only)	Solo motorcycles, only when necessary space is available on front fender	Front: left fender Rear: right fender or rear of vehicle	Front: left fender Rear: right side of tailgate or rear end.	Front: below the division emblem Rear: Right side of rear wall

Note: The terms "left" and "right" always seen in the direction of travel.

a)

b)

c)

d)

e)

f)

g)

h)

i)

j)

k)

l)

Identity markings of vehicles of the 1st Cossack Division with the division emblem:

a) H.Q 1st Cossack Cavalry Brigade
b) H.Q. 1st Cossack Division supply units and Reconnaissance Battalion 55
c) H.Q. 2nd Cossack Cavalry Brigade
d) Don Cossack Cavalry Regiment 1
e) Siberian Cossack Cavalry Regiment 2
f) Kuban Cossack Cavalry Regiment 3
g) Kuban Cossack Cavalry Regiment 4
h) Don Cossack Cavalry Regiment 5
i) Terek Cossack Cavalry Regiment 6
j) Cossack Pioneer Battalion
k) Cossack Signals Battalion
l) 1st and 2nd Mounted Cossack Artillery Battalion

General von Pannwitz's command vehicle. On the right fender is the tactical symbol of the division headquarters.

Cossacks in the *Wehrmacht*

Photographs of the Cossacks in Training and Combat

Mogilev, 1941-42. *Generalleutnant* von Schenkendorff and *Oberstleutnant* Kononov with Cossack Battalion 600, which later became the Don Cossack Cavalry Regiment 5. *Oberstleutnant* Kononov commanded Cossack Battalion 600.

Mogilev, winter 1942-43. *Rittmeister* Count Rittberg, Sonderführer Dr. Blaese and *Oberstleutnant* Kononov.

On the left is a German officer. Behind him is a Cossack officer, still in Russian uniform. The assembled Cossacks also wear various items of Russian clothing. They wear a white armband on the left upper sleeve as an identity marking.

Red Army rank badges are visible on this man's shirt collar. The three squares indicate a lieutenant. The Soviet star has been removed from the saddlecloth.

Mielau, 1943. Part of the camp occupied by the 3rd Cavalry Regiment Svodny (from 26 June 1943), which later became the Kuban Cossack Cavalry Regiment 3.

Potsdam-Krampnitz, early summer 1943. *Oberst* Kulakov, the Ataman of the Terek Cossacks (in the foreground, seated, wearing a cherkesska), with Cossacks visiting the Army Riding and Driving School. On the left is a Gefreiter wearing a cherkesska. At Krampnitz demonstrations were given for guests every Wednesday. Cossacks were frequent visitors.

Mielau, about mid-1943. 3rd Cavalry Regiment Svodno (Svodny from 26 June 1943, Kuban Cossack Cavalry Regiment 3 from 5 Aug. 1943). German core personnel attached to the regimental headquarters. They wear the sleeve badge of the Kuban Cossacks on their upper left sleeves.

Mielau, 1943. The commander of the Kuban Cossack Cavalry Regiment 3, *Oberstleutnant* Jungschulz von Roebern (in leather coat), presents prizes after a regimental riding competition.

This young Cossack (center) also took part in the competition.

Mielau 1943. A mounted platoon of the Don Cossack Cavalry Regiment 5.

Mielau troop training grounds, 1943. Cossacks of the Don Cossack Cavalry Regiment 5 practice with mortars.

Mielau, September 1943. Some of the many Cossack troops assembled to greet General Krasnov.

The regimental commanders have also been assembled. On the extreme right the Ataman of the Terek Cossacks, *Oberst* Kulakov.

General Krasnov, *General* von Pannwitz and *Oberst* von Bosse.

General Krasnov and *Major* Pugovochnikov.

General Krasnov greets *Oberst* Kulakov. *Oberst* Kulakov and the officer next to him are wearing the cherkesska. On the left upper sleeve of *Oberst* Kulakov's cherkesska is the sleeve badge of the Terek Cossacks.

General Krasnov, *General* von Pannwitz and the division pope.

Shepetovka, Russia, 1943. The Cossack choir singing.

Cossack officers and members of the local population enjoy the singing.

Ilok, Slovenia, October 1943. From left: *Rittmeister* von Abel, brigade operations officer; *Oberst* Baron von Wolff, brigade commander (Don) I; *Generalmajor* von Pannwitz (with back to photographer), commander of the 1st Cossack Division; *Rittmeister* Schreiber, commander 1st Battalion, Siberian Cossack Cavalry Regiment 2; *Oberstleutnant* Baron von Nolcken, commander Siberian Cossack Cavalry Regiment 2.

Major Rojahn and Major Count zu Eltz.

General Shkuro greets a Wachtmeister of the Siberian Cossack Cavalry Regiment 2.

Croatia, 1943 or 1944. Generals Shkuro (1st from left) and Naumenko (2nd from left) visiting the 1st Cossack Division. Standing next to General Naumenko is *Generalmajor* von Pannwitz, while on the right of the photograph is *Oberst* Bosse, commander of the Cossack Cavalry Brigade (Caucasus) 2.

Left: *General* Shkuro and *General* Naumenko with officers of the 1st Cossack Division.

Croatia, 1943-44. Don Cossack Cavalry Regiment 5. From the left: Dr. Blaese, *Rittmeister* Pashchenko, *Oberleutnant* Mazuhn and Zahlmeister Gartner. Note the variety of collar patches: specialist (Sonderführer), Cossack officers, army officers and army civilian officials of officer rank.

German and Cossack members of the 1st Cossack Division. These men are carrying an interesting variety of weapons: a Russian Nagant 95 revolver (extreme left, in holster), a Russian PP D 40 submachine-gun (back row), a Russian PPsh-41 submachine-gun (front row), a German MG 42 (front row), and a shashka.

Group photograph following the inspection of the Don Cossack Cavalry Regiment 5 by the army administrator of Army Group E in Agram in December 1944. The two Cossacks (left and right) are armed with German MP 40 submachine-guns.

Rittmeister Borisenkov (Don Cossack Cavalry Regiment 5).

Oberstleutnant Wagner (left) and *General* von Pannwitz (center) with the chetniks in Doboy.

Oberstleutnant Aleksiç and Ustacha leader Paget on one of the Save ferries.

Yugoslavia. *Generalleutnant* von Pannwitz on a ride with Cossacks of the Guard Troop on the bank of the Save River.

Yugoslavia, late November 1944. The Cossack regiments march from Djakovo to Sisak.

Serbia, 1944. Officers of the Kuban Cossack Cavalry Regiment 3. Left: *Rittmeister* Langfeldt, commander of the 2nd Battalion. Second from the left is *Oberstleutnant* Jungschulz von Roebern, the regimental commander.

Sisak, Croatia, 14 February 1944. Burial of fallen members of the Division Reconnaissance Battalion 55.

Agram, 18 March 1944. At the Jelliacie Monument: in the foreground, from the left: *General* Glaise von Horstenau, *Generalleutnant* von Pannwitz, *Oberst* von Bosse, *Oberstleutnant* Baron P. Wolff and *Major* Count zu Eltz. Right: the Kuban Cossack Cavalry Regiment 4 marches past the Jelliacie Monument.

Oberst von Selchow, *Major* Rojahn, *Generalleutnant* von Pannwitz, *General* Glaise von Horstenau and *Major* Count zu Eltz after the marchpast.

Major Erwein Karl Count zu Eltz, the intelligence officer of the 1st Cossack Division and the XV Cossack Cavalry Corps.

Croatia October 1944. Andrei, an orphan, as a member of the Young Cossacks with the Don Cossack Cavalry Regiment 5. In his right hand he holds an Italian Carcano Model 38 carbine.

Croatia, 1944. On the left the commander of the 2nd Battalion of the Kuban Cossack Cavalry Regiment 3, *Rittmeister* (and Knight's Cross wearer) Kay Langfeldt.

Croatia, Easter 1944. 2nd Battalion, Kuban Cossack Cavalry Regiment 3. Ethnic Germans serving as interpreters.

Summer 1944. *Generalleutnant* von Pannwitz reviews the Guard Troop in the park in Chernik. Following him are Majors Himmighofen (on right with peaked cap) and Weil (with mountain cap).

Cossacks during their free time.

Croatia, spring 1944. A Cossack troop enjoys a garden party with residents of a village. The men are from the Don Cossack Cavalry Regiment 5.

In the combat zone around Banya Luka. On the left *Oberleutnant* Kraus, in the center *Oberst* Kononov and *General* von Pannwitz, extreme right *Oberst* von Schultz.

Yugoslavia, April 1944. Cossacks of the Don Cossack Cavalry Regiment 1 during a rest stop. Note the broad red stripe on the breeches of the man in the center of the photograph.

The Cossacks knew nothing of German-style riding schools, but they lived with horses from the time they could walk and were excellent riders, guiding their horses by shifting weight and using the nagaika (whip). Riding games, called djshigitovka, were much loved by the Cossacks.

Test of obedience for the horses. Cossacks using their horses as cover.

Yugoslavia. Oberstabsarzt Dr. Grass (division medical officer of the 1st Cossack Division) and *Oberstleutnant* Lehmann, commander of the Kuban Cossack Cavalry Regiment 3 from February 1944.

General von Pannwitz and *Oberleutnant* Count Stolberg.

Photograph taken in Austria on 9 or 10 May 1945. The Cossacks have formed up for morning roll call in their prisoner of war camp. In the group on the left may be seen a female Cossack medic. The German national emblems have been removed from their uniforms. The sad fate of thousands of Cossacks was about to begin.

Bibliography

Angolia, J.R. LTC (Ret.): *Belt Buckles and Brocades*, USA 1982

Angolia, J.R. LTC (Ret.) and Schlicht, *Adolf: Uniforms and Traditions of the German Army 1933-1945*, Vol. 2, USA 1986

Ausky Stanislav: „Olaf Jordan, ein Maler zwischen den Kosaken". In: *Nachrichten der Kameradschaft des XV. Kos.-Kav.-Korps*, Nr. 52/1986 und 53/1987

Carnier, Pier Arrigo: *L'armata cosacca in Italia 1944-1945*, Mailand 1990

Eltz, Erwein-Karl Graf zu: *Mit den Kosaken*, Donaueschingen 1970

Greehey, William H.: The german XVth Cossack Cavalry Corps. In: *Adjutant's Call*, Journal of the Military Historical Society, 1967, USA

Hoffmann, Joachim: *Deutsche und Kalmyken*, Freiburg 1974

Hoffmann, Joachim: *Die Ostlegionen*, Freiburg 1976

Hoffmann, Joachim: *Kaukasien 1942/43*, Freiburg 1991

Oberst a.D. Kalben, Heinrich-Detloff von, und Oberst a.D. Wagner, *Constantin: Die Geschichte des XV. Kosaken-Kavallerie-Korps*, Hrsg. Kameradschaft des XV. Kos.-Kav.-Korps, 1989

Kern, Erich: *General von Pannwitz und seine Kosaken*, Pr. Oldendorf 1971

Klietmann, Dr. K.G.: *Fahnen und Flaggen der 1. Kos.-Div.*, Heft 28 „Die deutsche Wehrmacht 1934-1945", Verlag die Ordenssammlung, Berlin 1964

Klietmann Dr. K.G.: *Auszeichnungen des Deutschen Reiches 1936-1945*, Stuttgart 1981

Littlejohn, David: *Foreign Legions of the Third Reich*, Vol. 4, San Jose 1987

Martin, Walter: *Die Geschichte der Kosaken*, Stein/Österreich 1986

Neulen, Hans Werner: *An deutscher Seite*. Internationale Freiwillige von Wehrmacht und Waffen-SS, München 1985

Oertle, Vinzenz: Das XV. *Kosaken-Kavallerie-Korps*. In Heft 26 „Der Tanzbödler", Oetwil am See/Schweiz 1989

Rottmann, Hans: *Die russische Armee*, Leipzig o.J.

Tolstoy, Nikolai: *Die Verratenen von Jalta*, München/Wien 1977

Wenzel, Edgar M.: *So gingen die Kosaken durch die Hölle*, 1976 Wien

Wagner, Eduard: *Hieb- und Stichwaffen*, Prag 1966

Notes

Notes

Notes

Notes